THE BEST
BIKE RIDES
IN
TEXAS

THE BEST BIKE RIDES IN TEXAS

by

Andy White

Foreword by

Lance Armstrong

A Voyager Book

Old Saybrook, Connecticut

Library of Congress Cataloging-in-Publication Data

White, Andy (Andrew S.)
  The best bike rides in Texas / by Andy White ; foreword by Lance Armstrong. — 1st ed.
      p.   cm. — (Best bike rides series)
  "A Voyager book."
  Includes index.
  ISBN 1-56440-735-7
  1. Bicycle touring—Texas—Guidebooks.   2. Texas—Guidebooks.
I. Title.   II. Series.
GV1045.5.T4W45   1995

                                                        95-32863
                                                           CIP

Dedicated to the memory of Patricia E. Rant
1947–1995
an adventurous traveler who loved travel books.
Her special grace will be remembered by her many friends.

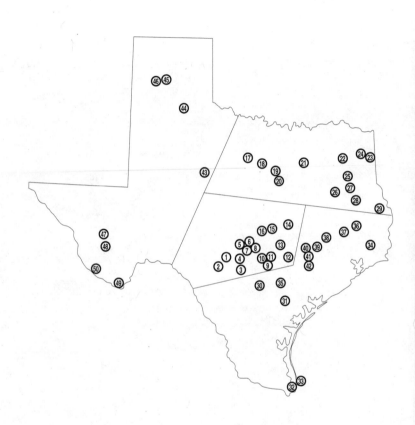

Contents

Foreword

by Lance Armstrong

I started riding bicycles as a teenager so that I could compete in triathlons. I'm motivated by the thrill of competition and the desire to win, and for that I've always loved cycling. Now I ride my bike for a living, and when I ride, whether it's from my home in Texas or during the racing season in Europe, I ride to train and compete.

The excitement of competition and desire to win are my motivations for riding a bicycle, but they aren't the only reasons to ride. Almost everyone can enjoy cycling at their own speed and in their own way. The roads of my home state are a great place for this.

I come back to central Texas each year after the racing season ends to relax, enjoy the company of my friends, and benefit from all the special things this area has to offer. I've lived in Texas all my life, and I moved to Austin as soon as I could once I began devoting my full time and efforts to cycling. I'm always glad to be here, and I look forward to returning when I'm away.

My team, sponsored by Motorola, is made up of professional cyclists from around the world. This year, Motorola brought them all to Austin for a winter training camp. It was a terrific opportunity to get these young riders together to start our training, have some fun, and begin coming together as a team.

Motorola chose Texas as the site for our winter camp independently of me, and other cycling programs have chosen Texas as a training site as well. When I competed as an amateur prior to the 1992 Olympics, our national team held two winter camps in the Texas Hill Country. Mild weather and empty roads made it a good place for us to train.

I've taken my friends and teammates cycling on many of my favorite Texas routes. Some of the roads heading west from Austin toward Marble Falls have a magical quality for me. I enjoy the roads through the hills around Wimberley, to the southwest of Austin, as well.

This winter I took my Canadian teammate Steve Bauer for a hard workout on the roads leading toward Marble Falls. Steve likes to measure changes in altitude on his rides with the altimeter in his watch, and on this ride it recorded more than 6,000 feet of vertical climbing along the way! Later I remembered that this same unreliable altimeter indicated we were more than 1,000 feet below sea level when we rode the train through the "chunnel" between France and England during the 1994 Tour de France. Still, a ride along the roads toward in Marble Falls can be especially challenging.

Rides like these serve my purposes, but you don't have to be training for professional races to enjoy cycling on Texas roads. What's important isn't always how far or how fast or how hard you ride, but that, in your own way and at your own speed, you get out and enjoy the best bike rides in Texas. You'll find suggestions to help you not only in this book, but from friends, other riders, organized biking events, or a local bike shop as well. Use all these sources to put together rides that are suited for you.

When Andy and I talked about our favorite places to bike in Texas, several roads that one or the other of us haven't yet tried came up. Even though we both ride often here, this was no surprise. There's always a new route to try or another area to explore in this huge state, and that's part of what makes cycling in Texas unique and special.

So are the people of Texas, who in my experience are especially accommodating and friendly. There are lots of Texans who enjoy cycling, and we're used to seeing bicycles on Texas roads. Although you'll always remember that occasional unfriendly motorist who can cross your path no matter where you ride, I find cycling in Texas is a pleasure, especially compared to my experiences with traffic in Europe.

Texas has always been my home, and I expect it always will be. I encourage you to come cycle its roads and meet its people.

Lance Armstrong is one of America's most accomplished professional cyclists. He is the 1993 World Champion and has claimed victories in prestigious races throughout Europe and the United States, including the 1995 Tour du Pont and stages of the Tour de France. Lance was born and raised in Texas and lives in Austin during the off-season.

Lance Armstrong

Introduction

The Best Bike Rides in Texas

Welcome to *The Best Bike Rides in Texas*. There are wonderful experiences waiting for you on bike rides along the roads of the Lone Star State.

This book is about seeing Texas by bicycle. Whether your travels through Texas take you to new or familiar locales, the view from your bicycle will offer a unique perspective of this enormous and colorful state.

Size and diversity are Texas hallmarks. A rich natural and cultural heritage exists within its boundaries. From lush forests to arid deserts, mountain peaks to sandy beaches, Texas supports a variety and style of life found nowhere else.

Happily, Texas is as accessible as it is vast. An excellent network of roads blankets the state, connecting people and places across an area large enough to fit fifteen of the fifty states within its borders at once and still have a thousand square miles left over.

Bicycle travel on Texas roads offers special rewards. For cyclists, Texas roads connect more than merely the towns they pass through.

A bike ride on Texas roads connects cyclists to the surrounding countryside and the wildlife that inhabits it. You'll get a closer, more intimate look at and feel for a variety of birds, animals, wildflowers, and geology almost too diverse to catalog.

A bike ride on Texas roads connects cyclists with earlier travelers along the same paths, the cultures these travelers brought with them, and the legacies they left behind. You'll add your own adventures and efforts to the discoveries and struggles that took place along these routes generations ago.

A bike ride on Texas roads connects cyclists with friends and people met along the way through shared experiences and memories. You'll learn a lot about your companions and about yourself during the time you spend cycling here.

There are as many ways to enjoy cycling in Texas as there are great places to ride. Whether you prefer to ride alone or with others, continuing uninterrupted over long distances or stopping frequently over short stretches, there is plenty to see and do while cycling here. Use this book to help you enjoy the best bike rides in Texas in the way best suited to you.

How to Use This Book

About the Routes

The fifty routes in The Best Bike Rides in Texas are divided into four categories according to degree of difficulty. These classifications are subjective, taking into account the combination of distance, road grade, and bike-handling skills necessary to negotiate the full tour. Each route's name indicates its relative degree of difficulty.

Rambles are the least demanding of the routes. Most are between fifteen and twenty-five miles in length, with only two Rambles traveling as far as thirty miles. Rambles generally cross flat or gently rolling terrain on lightly traveled roads or roads with adequate shoulders where traffic is heavier.

Cruises contain one or two features for those more familiar with bicycle touring. Most Cruises are between thirty and forty miles long, and portions may have difficult hills or some traffic. The fifteen-mile ride through Palo Duro Canyon is rated as a Cruise because of the cycling skills needed to control the steep, twisting descent into the canyon and the physical conditioning needed to conquer the long climb out.

Challenges are designed for riders who have developed the physical conditioning and have the experience to confidently cycle longer distances. Covering forty to sixty miles, Challenges can contain steep climbs and long stretches through remote country.

Classics are recommended only for experienced, well-conditioned cyclists. The seven Classics in this book range from sixty to one hundred miles in length over the most difficult terrain in Texas. The steepest grades on Texas highways are covered in the Classics along routes that demand careful preparation and advanced cycling skills to negotiate.

Many of the route descriptions contain specific options to shorten or suggestions to lengthen a ride. Each route classification is based on the difficulty of the full tour. Appendix D contains a mileage table listing the option distances described in each route.

Don't let the distance of a longer tour dissuade you from trying a ride in an attractive area. Out-and-back rides along portions of a route or the shorter options provided may be well suited to you. Likewise, don't dismiss a shorter ride in an interesting spot. In a few locations, two tours share a common starting point and can be combined for a longer ride.

In each route narrative directions include the cumulative mileage to each turn and to significant landmarks along the way. It's possible that your mileage may differ slightly from the mileage listed in these narratives. Over enough miles, differences in odometer calibration, tire pressure, and the line you follow can have an impact on the measurement of distance. Use the cumulative mileage in connection with your route descriptions and maps.

The selection of these route locations is the result of extensive research and reading; suggestions from bicycle shops, cycling friends, and local experts; and twenty years of experience cycling Texas roads. Some of the locations are popular and well-known cycling venues; others are less frequently visited by bike riders. Taken as a whole, the routes in this book are meant to offer a cross section of the best bike riding locations in the state, indicative of the wide variety of Texas roads and terrain.

To the greatest extent possible, each route has been designed with specific criteria in mind, though all of them could not be fully addressed in every instance. Starting points should be easy to find, with convenient public parking and access to provisions. Roads should be moderately traveled, be in good repair, and have adequate shoulders when traffic volume requires. Routes should be directed to pass available stores at useful intervals. Routes also should contain interesting things to see or do along the way or have an interesting story to tell based on the people or places passed.

To fashion the most useful routes, some worthwhile features were bypassed for practical considerations. As a result, you might find it appropriate to use these routes as starting points and/or suggestions in designing your own best bike rides. Rides can begin at any point along the course described in the route directions. You can leave the course to explore interesting side roads and create your own routes.

Construction, development, improvements, and changes are constantly taking place on Texas roadways. As a result, the route descriptions and maps in this book can only be records of conditions as they once were; they may not always be descriptive of the conditions as you find them. Comments from interested and critical readers are appreciated by an author who wants to keep this book current and useful. I'd be grateful to learn of any changes or discrepancies you encounter.

Texas Roads

The open road occupies a cherished place in Texas culture, and the ability to drive to almost any point in this giant state seems taken for granted. Each year large sums of money are spent on the construction and upkeep of the state's highway system. Cyclists in Texas benefit greatly from the justifiable pride Texans take in these high-quality roadways.

The 300,000-mile road network in Texas is the largest of any state in America. More than 70,000 of these miles are part of the state-maintained highway system. Not all the roads in Texas make for good cycling, but most of Texas is accessible by bicycle.

A unique Texas feature is a system of more than 40,000 miles of rural routes marked as farm-to-market, ranch-to-market, and ranch-to-ranch roads. These are generally lightly traveled, two-lane roads that often pass through beautiful parts of the Texas countryside. As much as possible, the routes in this book are designed to utilize these farm and ranch roads.

The farm-and-ranch road network was developed for bringing

crops and livestock from outlying areas into towns. There's no difference between a farm road and a ranch road other than farm roads are in farming areas and ranch roads are in ranch territory. Across the long distances of west Texas, some roads link ranches to each other rather than to a town and are designated as ranch-to-ranch roads.

The roads in the state-maintained highway system, along with most county-maintained roads, are identified by a number. All roads in the state highway system also are identified on roadway signs by a distinctive symbol that encloses the road's number. Throughout this book abbreviations are used to designate roads in the state highway system as follows:

Roadway (abbreviation): Symbol on Roadway Sign

- US Highways (US): Black or red shield
- Texas Highways (Texas): White square or circle with black border
- Farm-to-Market (FM): White Texas silhouette on black background
- Ranch-to-Market (RM): White Texas silhouette on black background
- Ranch Road (RR): White Texas silhouette on black background

Other roads, including interstate highways (IH), state park roads, county roads, and platted roads, are identified in this book by their name or number.

The Texas Department of Transportation is a terrific source of maps and travel and tourist information. *Texas Highways* magazine is an excellent publication full of facts and insight about Texas roads. There are regional offices throughout the state; you can call their travel and information division in Austin (800–452–9292) for assistance.

In the mid-1970s, the Texas Department of Transportation developed ten "travel trails" along roads in the state highway system to promote the unique character and history of certain areas. Many of the routes in this book cross roads designated by blue-and-white rectangular signs as a part of a travel trail. Often a reference to these signs, marking a route as part of the Texas Independence Trail, the Texas Forest Trail, or one of the other travel trails, will be made in the "Miles & Directions" section of a route narrative. Call or write the travel and information division for area maps of these travel trails, complete with descriptions of points of interest along the way.

Maps

Good maps make all the difference when exploring a new area by bicycle. A special thanks to Clinton Phillips for his work on the maps in this book. Clinton is a graduate student in the geography department of the University of Texas.

Space considerations prevent the inclusion of more detail in each of Clinton's maps. If you are cycling in an unfamiliar area or exploring new roads in a familiar area, it may be helpful to have maps with as much detail of your surroundings as possible.

The best and most detailed county maps are prepared by the Texas Department of Transportation. These maps are reasonably priced and are updated regularly. You can buy an entire set of county maps, individual county maps, or maps of segments of the more densely developed Texas counties. Call the map sales office in Austin (512–465–7397) for more information.

Shearer Publishing publishes an excellent Texas atlas called *The Roads of Texas,* which is available in most bookstores. They have a toll free number (800–458–3808) as well. This atlas contains a great deal of useful travel information.

The routes in this book were researched from maps provided by local bike shops, book stores, and area chambers of commerce. Most state and national park facilities maintain maps of the roads through their parks. Supplement the maps in this book with all these resources.

Elevation profiles are included for each Classic route. Measurements for these profiles come from U.S. Geological Survey maps kept at the University of Texas.

Texas Parks

The Census Bureau lists more than 80 percent of Texans as urban residents, yet a rural heritage is deeply ingrained in the lives and character of most Texans. Recreation and the outdoors is a prized part of Texas's past and present.

Much of this special heritage is on display in the extraordinary state parks, natural areas, and historic sites maintained by the Texas Parks and Wildlife Department. These facilities vary widely in size and setting and in historic, natural, and cultural significance. They also provide some of the best locations for bicycle riding anywhere in the state.

Several of the more than 130 sites that currently comprise the Texas state park system are featured in this book as starting points or points of interest along a route. Texas Parks and Wildlife employees are especially accommodating and welcoming to all types of cyclists, including off-road riders, long-distance tourists, and families. Park roads are generally quiet, safe, well marked, and traveled by other visitors in a recreation frame of mind. The parks are often in beautiful settings with plenty of interesting features to explore before or after a ride.

Schedules and rules regarding use and operation of the parks vary with each site. Most state parks require entrance fees, and there may be parking or activity fees depending upon the nature of the facility you visit. Texas Parks and Wildlife maintains a toll-free general information number (800–792–1112) to help plan trips throughout the park system.

Texas parks are very popular, and reservations for certain activities are advised. Texas Parks and Wildlife has a central reservation center for bookings of most of the tours, activities, camping, and group facilities available throughout the park system. A call to the reservation center (512–389–8900) will make planning a trip to a state park area more efficient.

Other routes in this book visit facilities maintained by the National Park Service, including national parks, national forests, national wildlife refuges, and a national seashore. Appendix D provides a list of routes that visit a state or national park facility, along with a table of route mileages.

Special Considerations for Cycling in Texas

A special Texas style and outlook can turn the otherwise ordinary into something memorable and different. As a result, there are some circumstances and situations unique to cycling in Texas. To maximize your enjoyment and safety, be prepared to encounter some or all of the following on your bike rides:

Cattle guards. Cattle and other livestock are raised in every part of Texas, and many rural Texas roads pass through open, unfenced range and pastureland. Cattle guards are a common feature along such roads. Cattle guards are often placed in a roadway where a ranch or pasture boundary is crossed to keep livestock from wandering off private property.

A cattle guard is a row of metal bars laid across a road in a trough cut into the road surface. On occasion a bar is not firmly set or is placed a few inches higher or lower than the road surface. Some bars have a gap in the center running parallel to the roadway. Loose gravel may surround the approach to some cattle guards. Cattle guards are just a few feet across, but they are deep enough to disrupt the passage of both livestock and bicycles.

Approach cattle guards with caution and keep the following in mind:

* **Cross perpendicular to the bars.** To lessen the chance that a wheel will slip between bars, choose a path for your bike that crosses the bars at a 90-degree angle. If a cattle guard is placed in or near a curve in the road, cross the bars as close to a 90-degree angle as possible, turning before or after, but not while, you ride over the bars.

* **Adjust your speed.** Depending on your bike-handling skills, crossing a cattle guard at a moderate speed may not be as rough as crossing at an extremely slow speed. When choosing your crossing speed, look ahead to see whether any beams are set slightly higher or lower than the road or if any beams are missing. Be especially at-

tentive to your speed on wet roads and where loose gravel surrounds a cattle guard. When in doubt, slow down.

* **Watch your tire pressure.** Before and during a ride involving cattle-guard crossings, check to ensure that your tires are properly inflated. This may lessen the risk of flat tires from encounters with these rougher surfaces.

Livestock, wild game, and other road users. Wild and domestic animals are common sights along many of the routes in this book. Herds of cattle, sheep, goats, deer, pigs, pronghorn antelope, and exotic game walk, run, and lounge along many of the country roads, providing a special dimension to a bike ride.

Always approach these animals with caution. They are easily startled and apt to run, alone or in a group, heedless of obstacles such as cyclists. Along with their beauty and grace, you may be amazed at the speed and power these animals can generate. Don't try to pass between animals or through a herd.

Not all the animals along Texas roadways are so attractive. Dogs may test your cycling skills from time to time. Ignore them or outrun them if you can, or try to deter some of the more persistent ones with shouts or a squirt from a water bottle. Buzzards will scatter at the sound of your approach. Let them hear you coming so that they'll have plenty of time to get out of the way.

Water crossings. Many rural Texas roads are built over creek beds that are usually dry but fill up quickly depending on rainfall. Other roads are intentionally constructed across a shallow stream as a "low-water crossing," so that a steady flow of water crosses the road. This is done so that the road doesn't alter or impede the water's course and flood private property. In either event you may find running water crossing a road and blocking your path.

Navigate these crossings with great caution. Although a crossing may appear shallow or still, constant exposure of a roadway to water usually leaves the submerged surface slippery, smooth, and often algae covered. Always dismount and walk your bike through water crossings. You'll be surprised how quickly your feet will dry off, especially in the heat of summer.

Private property. Private property is a serious subject in Texas, and respect for private property rights is a must when cycling along

Texas roads. Courtesy and consideration of the property of others will go a long way toward engendering goodwill and minimizing unpleasant experiences.

Some of the most beautiful roadways in this book are surrounded by privately owned land, which is usually clearly marked and identified as such. On some rides, such as the Willow City Ramble or the Two Gruene/River Road Cruises, you'll notice special pleas for respect of private property. In other places, simple postings or fences will be your only warning.

Always keep yourself and the things you carry with you on roadways, shoulders, and public property during your ride. If you know you're passing through private property, resist the temptation to cross fence lines or wander off into the surrounding countryside in search of that unique photo opportunity or picnic site.

The weather. Changes in Texas weather can be dramatic and extreme. Some of these changes are seasonal. Expect windy conditions early in the spring and fall. Also expect serious heat in the summer.

Other changes are not so predictable. Sudden rains can quickly flood small creek beds or saturated fields and spill over into roadways. When warm air from Mexico collides with northern cold fronts, violent weather can result in a very short time. Different parts of the state, at different latitudes and elevations, experience different weather patterns.

Always make attention to the season and the prevailing weather conditions part of your ride planning. Consider that as much as the distance you ride, the time you spend exposed to the elements will make demands on your strength and endurance and dictate the difficulty of your ride. Dress appropriately and cover yourself for protection from intense sun in summer, wind in spring and fall, and cold in winter.

Railroads. Many of the towns along the routes in this book exist only because of the development of railroads. Though railroads today are not the dominant mode of transportation they once were, Texas is still laced with both active and abandoned railroad lines.

It's less common to encounter moving trains on a ride, but it's very common to encounter railroad track crossings on rural roads.

Each railroad crossing is unique in size, character, marking, angle, and level of maintenance. As many of these railroad crossings as possible are identified in the "Miles & Directions" portion of each route description.

Cross railroad tracks carefully, minding all the same considerations you would when crossing a cattle guard.

Hunting season. Texans are passionate and serious when it comes to hunting. Throughout the fall and winter, different birds and animals are "in season" for hunters. These seasons are prescribed by Texas Parks and Wildlife and vary from year to year depending on the part of the state and the type of animal.

Hunting takes place on private property, not roadways. This should be a great incentive to stay off private property and confine your cycling to the public rights-of-way.

Hunters are also travelers and sportsmen who enjoy the same outdoors as cyclists. You're sure to encounter hunters throughout the state if you ride in the fall and winter. A cycling trip during hunting season can benefit from some advance planning. Hunters flock to the countryside during the hunting season and compete with other travelers for accommodations. You can get information on hunting activity by calling Texas Parks and Wildlife or a local chamber of commerce.

Top Ten Tips for a Safer and More Enjoyable Ride

No matter how often you ride, there are always new lessons to learn—and old lessons to relearn—regarding ways to make cycling safer and more enjoyable. Mental preparation, as well as physical preparation, is an important part of improving your cycling skills.

There is a wide range of advice and information available in print on all aspects of the cycling experience. The knowledgeable cyclists you meet at a good bike shop or active cycling club can make valuable and practical suggestions to enhance the quality of your rides. Filter what you read and hear through your own good judgment and common sense.

From the many important things to keep in mind when riding

or preparing for a ride, the following "top ten" list is offered for special consideration:

* **Buy the best helmet you can find, make sure it fits properly, and wear it whenever you ride.** Other items of specialized cycling apparel have a practical utility for safety and comfort. Eyeglasses shield sun, wind, dirt, and insects. Jerseys are longer in the back to cover you as you stretch over your bike, contain large pockets to carry useful items, and are made of materials that wick away sweat. Gloves facilitate your grip and cushion a tender area in a fall. Black lycra shorts minimize chafing and retain heat for sore muscles. Shoes with stiff soles lessen foot fatigue.

* **Eat and drink during your ride.** Eating before you get hungry and drinking before you become thirsty will do wonders to maintain your energy level. Bring adequate provisions, as portions of your ride may be far from assistance. Try some of the wide variety of specialty sports drinks and foods designed to quickly replenish your reserves.

* **Protect yourself from the elements.** Long exposure to the sun and wind can be as much of a drain on your energy as any challenging terrain. Proper consideration of temperature is important, so be aware of the time of day and time of year that you ride. If possible, dress so that you can add and subtract layers in response to changes in weather. Make liberal use of sunscreen.

* **Maintain your bicycle in good mechanical condition.** Be sure that your bike fits you properly and that you are comfortable on it. Over time a properly fitted bike will maximize your riding efficiency and minimize the potential for certain injuries. Inflate your tires and check your equipment before you begin a ride. Carry spare parts and tools for repairs.

* **Be attentive.** Try to anticipate road obstacles and related hazards. Pay attention to traffic noise and make eye contact with drivers whenever possible to minimize surprises. Be predictable and consistent, and let traffic and other riders around you know what you're about to do. Be considerate and ride defensively.

* **Obey traffic laws.** Rules of vehicular traffic apply equally to motor vehicles and to bicycles. Assert your right to be on the roadways with a bicycle, but be practical in recognizing the vulnerabil-

ity of a smaller, slower-moving bicycle among larger automobiles traveling at higher speeds. Always ride with traffic and use hand signals to convey your intentions.

   * **Learn how to change a flat tire.** Confidence in your ability to repair a flat will increase your cycling range and enable you to relax and enjoy a long ride. Talk to your bike shop about a liner for your tires to minimize the chance of smaller punctures.

   * **Ride with others.** It's nice to have others to share your interest and experience and motivate and challenge you to longer, faster, or more frequent rides. If you ride alone in remote locations, be sure to carry identification, and tell someone where you are going and when you expect to return.

   * **Put the gears to work.** Get comfortable with switching gears to match the terrain you're riding through, so that you can spin the pedals quickly with a minimum of stress on your joints and muscles. Develop and practice other energy-saving cycling techniques, such as drafting in the slipstream created by the cyclists you ride with.

   * **Have fun!** Choose your distances and routes carefully depending on your level of conditioning, comfort, and confidence. Know your limits and vary your cycling routine. There are lots of ways to enjoy a bike ride. Try them all.

Please Note

Nothing in this book should be substituted for your own good judgment and common sense in dealing with the risks and dangers inherent in riding a bicycle. Use this book as a starting point for your cycling adventures, but rely on your experience and judgment as you ride.

   Features described along these routes may have changed since this book was written. Let us know if you encounter changes to road and traffic conditions, if you find descriptions unclear, or if you have suggestions that could make future editions of this book more useful. Write in care of the publisher or by "e-mail" to txbikebook@aol.com.

Disclaimer

The Globe Pequot Press and the author assume no liability for accidents happening to, or injuries sustained by, readers who engage in the activities described in this book.

Central Texas
and the Hill Country

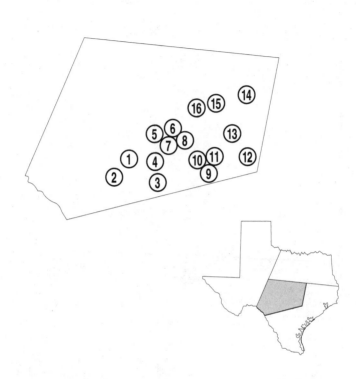

Central Texas and the Hill Country

1

Jeff Garvey's Favorite Hill Country Classic

Hunt—South Fork of the Guadalupe River—Garven's Store—North Fork of the Guadalupe River—Hunt

The north and south forks of the Guadalupe River converge in the small community of Hunt. Summer camps and ranches stocked with exotic game line the shores of these quiet river forks. Huge cypress trees border the river and contribute to the special character of this bike ride through the Texas Hill Country.

The post office next to the Hunt Store marks the starting point for this tour. Garven's Store, the only other store on this loop, marks the halfway point. In between is an area that for generations has been a popular summer recreation destination for Texas families. More recently, summer camps and ranches have begun hosting groups for retreats and other activities year-round, including a U.S. Cycling Federation winter training camp for its amateur national team members.

The first fifteen miles of the full tour follow the river's south fork over low-water crossings and past beautifully kept summer camps. The route then heads through open hill country to Garven's Store. A few miles after the store, you'll pass part of the Y.O. Ranch. A historical marker there describes the cattle drives from Kerr County ranches to stockyards in Kansas that continued until the 1940s. Most of the ranch land you'll ride past along this route still supports cattle raising, the production of mohair, and the hunting of exotic game. The final twelve miles follow the river's north fork past camps and ranch land filled with cypress, cedar, and live oak.

Don't let the distance of the full tour dissuade you from a visit to Hunt for a bike ride. An out-and-back of any distance along either fork of the river will be one of the nicest rides you'll ever take. This is an excellent route to ride at any time of the year, but it has a special character in the cooler months, when the air is crisp, the deer are running, and the countryside seems particularly peaceful.

The Basics

Start: From the post office in Hunt, one of the few buildings in the town. Hunt is 15 miles west of Kerrville on Texas 39. Look for parking around the post office, or ask about parking at the Hunt Store. There also may be parking at some public areas near the river along Texas 39 back toward Ingram.

Length: 67.2 miles. Shorter rides can be taken out-and-back along each fork of the Guadalupe River.

Terrain: Rolling hills.

Roads: Texas 39 and RM 1340 are quiet country roads; US 83 and Texas 41 carry higher-speed traffic but are lightly traveled and have ample shoulders.

Food: The Hunt Store; vending machine at the River Inn; Garven's Store is at mile 37.6.

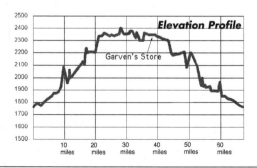

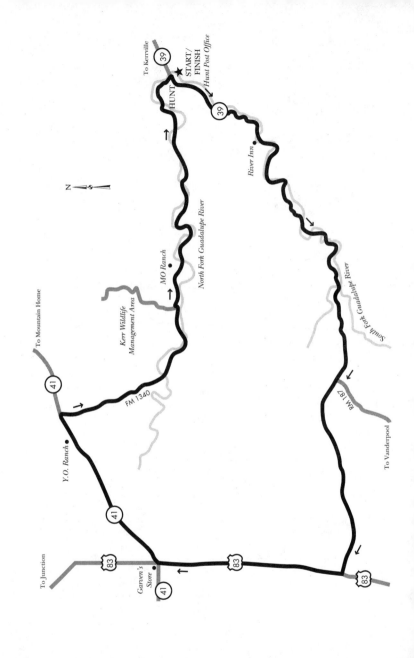

Miles & Directions

- 0.0 From the Hunt post office, ride west on Texas 39 along the South Fork of the Guadalupe River past a variety of cottages, inns, country residences, and summer camps.
- 6.6 Pass the River Inn. The soda machine there is your last opportunity to purchase a drink until Garven's Store (mile 37.6).
- 13.0 The road winds away from the river and into open hill country.
- 20.0 Continue straight on Texas 39 past the intersection with RM 187.
- 29.0 At the stop sign T intersection, turn right (north) onto US 83. Traffic is faster but light, and the shoulder is adequate.
- 37.6 Garven's Store is at the intersection of US 83 and Texas 41. Turn right (east) onto Texas 41. At mile 43.9 pass historical marker describing Y.O. Ranch history.
- 45.6 Turn right (south) onto FM 1340 across a cattle guard.
- 50.7 Begin to parallel the North Fork of the Guadalupe River. Pass Kerr wildlife management area at mile 54.4.
- 56.6 Pass the MO Ranch and go over an excellent river crossing. The remainder of the route passes by beautiful limestone bluffs, river crossings, and fields full of wild game.
- 65.2 Pass Stonehenge II, a replica of the ancient monument in England.
- 66.0 A historical marker at the Hunt/Japonica Cemetery relates local history.
- 67.1 At stop sign, turn right onto Texas 39. The two forks of the river merge nearby.
- 67.2 Finish at Hunt post office.

2

Lost Maples Challenge

Vanderpool—Leakey—Rio Frio—Utopia—Vanderpool

The canyons carved by the Sabinal and Frio rivers set the stage for a special bike ride. On this challenging tour you'll pass through all of the beauty that the Texas Hill Country has to offer.

The ride begins in Vanderpool at the Lost Maples General Store, which sits alone at the corner of RM 187 and RM 337. The folks at the store are very accommodating to cyclists, and if you're lucky, the stand out front that sells barbeque sandwiches will be open when you finish your ride.

This route begins immediately with a tremendous climb. Be prepared for, but don't be dissuaded by, the difficulty of the first few miles of the ride. Your reward will be breathtaking views of the Sabinal and Frio river valleys and thrilling descents to match the effort of your climb.

After the first, mountainous leg of this route, you'll cross the Frio River and enter the town of Leakey. The clear river waters and countryside filled with wild turkey, quail, dove, and other game have supported human habitation here since prehistoric times. Turning south along the Frio River, the canyon land gives way to gentler farmland and ranch land. An interesting historical marker past the community of Rio Frio describes how water was first brought to irrigate these lands.

The route approaches, but does not enter, Garner State Park, one of the most popular public campgrounds in Texas. Instead, you'll turn east over a long, open stretch of rolling hill country toward the town of Utopia. The last leg of your journey from Utopia repeatedly crosses the Sabinal River on the way back to Vanderpool.

Lost Maples State Natural Area draws fans of fall foliage from across the state, and a walk among the bigtooth maples lining the banks of the Sabinal River here is a must. You can add eight miles to the tour by starting at the park, but parking is limited, especially when the maples change color in November. If you are inclined to combine your bike ride with some camping, you'll be hard pressed to find better spots anywhere in Texas than the Lost Maples and Garner state parks. Be sure to call ahead for reservations if you're planning a stay at Garner in the summer or at Lost Maples in the fall.

The Basics

Start: From the Lost Maples General Store at the intersection of RM 187 and RM 337, 4 miles past the entrance to Lost Maples State Natural Area and 1 mile before the town of Vanderpool. The store owners welcome cyclists, but ask anyway before parking here. There is also parking at the post office in Vanderpool.

Length: 49.4 miles. Starting at the Lost Maples State Natural Area adds 8 miles.

Terrain: Long, steep climbs to start the tour, with equally dramatic descents following. Rolling hills on RM 1050. Otherwise fairly level.

Roads: Lightly traveled country roads. US 83 (used for 0.7 mile) has four lanes and an adequate shoulder.

Food: The Lost Maples General Store; several options in Leakey and Utopia.

Miles & Directions

- 0.0 From the Lost Maples General Store, head west on RM 337 toward Leakey and begin climbing almost immediately.
- 2.1 At the top of the first climb is a rest area with a nice view.

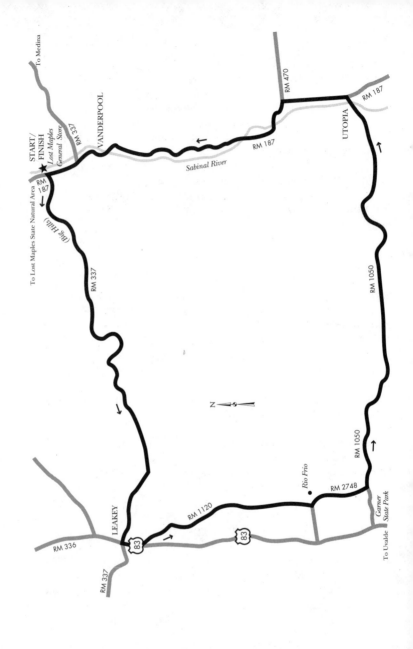

Don't be discouraged by the climb; the descent and the rest of this route are well worth the effort.

- 5.2 Begin another long, 1.5-mile climb.
- 14.5 Cross the Frio River and enter Leakey. A historical marker at the Leakey cemetery (mile 15.0) describes some area history.
- 15.1 Turn left (south) at the stop sign onto US 83. Convenience store at the corner.
- 15.8 Turn left onto RM 1120.
- 21.5 Pass through the community of Rio Frio.
- 22.0 At intersection with RM 2748, bear left (south). A historical marker here recounts the settlement of this area.
- 24.1 At stop sign, turn left (east) onto RM 1050. RM 1050 crosses rolling terrain with some climbing. You'll be more exposed to the wind and sun.
- 37.5 Cross the Sabinal River and enter Utopia. There will be several more crossings of the Sabinal River on the rest of the route.
- 37.7 At the stop sign turn left (north) onto RM 187. There are several stores in Utopia.
- 40.1 Stay on RM 187 as it bears left at the intersection with RM 470.
- 48.4 Pass through Vanderpool.
- 49.4 Finish at the Lost Maples General Store.

3

Bandera Classic

Bandera—Medina—Vanderpool—
Utopia—Tarpley—Bandera

It's less than an hour's drive from San Antonio to Bandera, a small town with the look and feel of the Old West. Bandera is surrounded by working and guest ranches, where cookouts, rodeos, and trail rides are a part of everyday life.

Bandera also sits on the edge of a remote and magnificent part of Texas. The Hill Country is more like mountain country here, particularly along a spectacular stretch between Medina and Vanderpool. As a result, this is one of the most difficult—and most rewarding—routes to ride in this book.

The ride starts out innocently enough through pastureland with distant glimpses into the Hill Country. There are vistas of mountains as you head toward Medina, but the route seems at first to turn away from the steeper terrain. The real challenge begins after leaving Medina, so be sure your water bottles are full on the way through town.

After Medina the grades increase steadily, and the hillsides slowly close in on the road. Before long you're riding through a very special part of the Texas Hill Country, over beautiful river and creek crossings, past huge limestone bluffs and cliffs, through green valleys, and toward rugged, desolate hills. After crossing Duncan Creek you'll be battling mountainous terrain and enjoying summit views all the way to Vanderpool.

The Lost Maples General Store is less than a mile to the right where the route turns left in Vanderpool. Likewise, there are stores two miles to the right where the route turns left again in Utopia. You'll want to consider a visit to one of these two spots, as the only other store on the last thirty miles of the ride is a small place in Tarpley called Howdy's. With luck, they'll be open when you pass by.

The stretch between Vanderpool and Utopia is relatively flat, with repeated crossings of the beautiful Sabinal River. This portion of the route, traveling in the other direction, is also found on the **Lost Maples Challenge.** The return from Utopia to Bandera has the same mountain challenges and remote character of the route's beginning. The entire route displays terrific fall colors but is beautiful to ride at any time of the year. Hill Country elevations make it a little cooler and dryer in this part of Texas.

This route is extremely popular with serious long-distance cyclists. The Ultra Marathon Cycling Association, whose members seek out lengthy rides over difficult terrain, combines this route with the **Lost Maples Challenge** for a route of 107 miles they've dramatically named the "Leakey Death Ride." It is one of the ultimate one-day cycling challenges in Texas.

The Basics

Start: At the Bandera County courthouse, from the corner of Main St. and Pecan St. There is public parking around the courthouse. Bandera is 50 miles west of San Antonio on Texas 16.
Distance: 73.9 miles.
Terrain: Hilly to mountainous, among the most difficult in this book. There is a beautiful flat section between Vanderpool and Utopia in the middle of the route.
Roads: Light traffic on FM roads. Some traffic on Texas 16 (used for 2.6 miles). The return from Utopia to Bandera is very lightly traveled, almost isolated.
Food: Lots of choices in Bandera; the Cider Mill in Medina as well as a few soda machines in front of other stores; the Lost Maples General Store is 1 mile off the route in Vanderpool; several stores 2 miles off the route in Utopia; a small store in Tarpley.

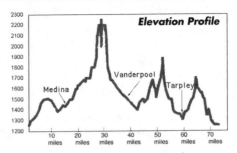

Miles & Directions

- **0.0** Head north on Main St., also called Texas 16 and Texas 173, from the corner of Pecan St.
- **0.3** Turn right (north) on Texas 173 where it diverges from Texas 16 at the stoplight.
- **0.8** Turn left (west) onto Ridge Route Rd., also named FM 3240.
- **8.0** Turn left (west) at stop sign T intersection onto RM 2828.
- **11.4** Turn right (north) on Texas 16 (2 lanes, flat, some traffic, no shoulder).
- **13.1** Enter Medina; pass a few stores with soda machines as well as the Cider Mill and Country Store, in the next mile.
- **14.0** Turn left (west) onto RM 337, crossing the Medina River and heading toward the mountains. This is a lovely section, with creek crossings, limestone cliffs, and outcroppings. Very hilly.
- **26.0** Cross Duncan Creek and start a steep 1-mile climb, followed by 3 miles of up and down along the top of the "Ridge Route."
- **29.7** Begin a long, steep descent with great views.
- **34.3** At stop sign T intersection, turn left (south) onto RM 187 at Vanderpool. The next 8 miles are fairly flat, with beautiful crossings of the Sabinal River.

The Lost Maples General Store is to the right here, on RM 337 in 1.1 miles.

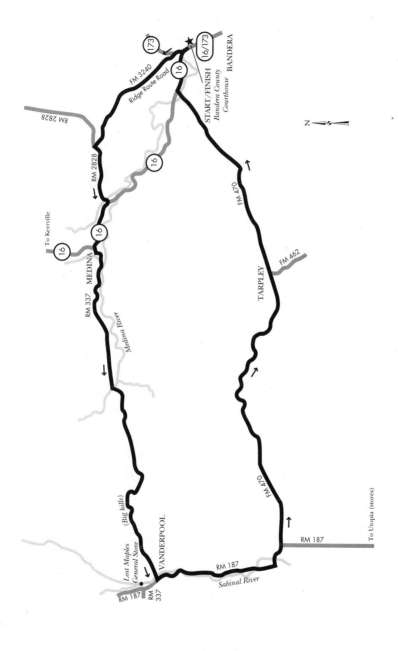

■ 42.5 Turn left (east) onto FM 470.

You'll find stores in Utopia if you continue straight on RM 187 for 2 miles.

■ 51.0 Begin long, steep climbs toward increasingly rolling terrain past great scenery. The terrain flattens out briefly near Tarpley.
■ 59.3 Enter Tarpley and pass small store on the right.
■ 71.3 Cross Medina River and turn right (south) at stop sign T intersection with Texas 16, which has a shoulder here. Texas 16 is marked as part of the Texas Hill Country Trail.
■ 73.6 Continue straight through the stoplight at the junction of Texas 173.
■ 73.9 Finish in front of the Bandera County courthouse.

4

Kerr County Cruise

Kerrville—Camp Verde—Center Point—Kerrville

Kerrville is the Hill Country's largest town and one of the state's premier resort and retirement centers. There always seems to be something of interest happening in or around Kerrville. The bluegrass and folk music festivals held on the Memorial Day and Labor Day weekends have become Texas institutions. Nearby summer camps and retreats host a variety of activities year-round.

Kerr County is popular with cyclists, and cyclists have been well received in Kerr County. Kerr County roads have been the site of amateur and professional races, informal group rides, and large organized tours. You'll notice a number of highway signs advising motorists of the presence of cyclists on some of the busier roads throughout the route described here, which travels south of Kerrville.

Kerr County is an excellent base for an extended cycling tour of the Hill Country. Over twenty years ago, the Lubbock Bicycle Club began bringing their members for informal tours of the area over a couple of days each spring. Gradually their Easter Hill Country Tour became known to riders from all over Texas, and today it is one of the most popular road rallies of the year. Bicycle clubs from Houston, Fort Worth, and San Antonio now take turns with the Lubbock club in hosting this event. Their rides have fanned out in all directions from Kerrville, including some of the roads on this route. Schreiner College, the starting point for this Cruise, is the starting point for much of the Easter Hill Country Tour.

Kerrville was settled in the 1840s by shingle makers drawn by the abundance of cypress trees in the area. The huge cypress trees that still line the rivers and creeks throughout this ride give portions of it a special feel. This course travels through a variety of terrain, so be prepared for quick changes in the character of the countryside and the roads. There are plenty of hills on this course as well as flats along rivers and creeks. There are some narrow, isolated roads as well as wider roads with higher-speed traffic.

Leaving the grounds of Schreiner College, the course crosses the Guadalupe River and travels south through neighborhoods and along state highways to Camp Verde, a crossroads established as an army outpost just prior to the Civil War. From Camp Verde the course turns east and makes several crossings of Verde Creek before reaching the small town of Center Point. From Center Point the course turns north and follows the Guadalupe River along back roads on the return to Kerrville.

The Basics

Start: At Schreiner College, on Texas 27 about 2 miles east of the Kerr County courthouse. Kerrville is about 70 miles west of San Antonio on I-10.

Distance: 33.2 miles.

Terrain: Hilly with some challenging climbs. Terrain is gentler between Camp Verde and Center Point and along River Rd.

Roads: Busy traffic on Texas 27 (first and last mile) and Texas 173, which have wide lanes but no shoulder. Texas 16 has high-speed traffic but a wide shoulder. FM roads are two lanes with lighter traffic. Country roads (Wharton, River, and West Creek) are narrow lanes with little traffic.

Food: Lots of options in Kerrville; interesting general store in Camp Verde; store in Center Point.

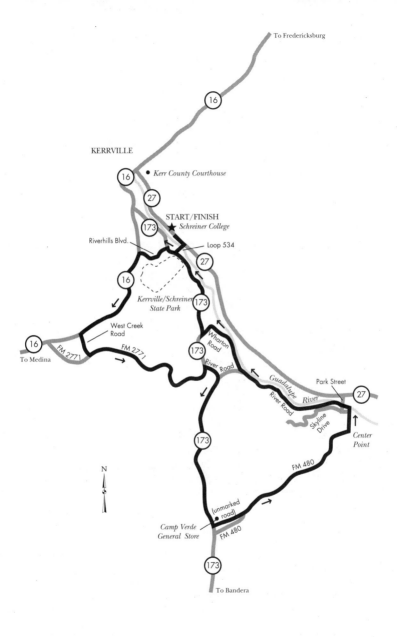

To Fredericksburg

16

KERRVILLE

16   • Kerr County Courthouse

27

173   START/FINISH
★ Schreiner College

Riverhills Blvd.   Loop 534

27

16

Kerrville/Schreiner   173
State Park

West Creek
Road   Wharton
Road

16   173
FM 2771   FM 2771   River Road

To Medina   River Road   Park Street

Guadalupe River   27

River Road

Skyline Drive   Center
Point

173   FM 480

N

(unmarked
• road)

Camp Verde   FM 480
General Store

173

To Bandera

Miles & Directions

- 0.0 Exit Schreiner College to the left (east) onto Texas 27, carefully crossing lanes of traffic.
- 1.0 At stoplight turn right (south) on Loop 534, across Guadalupe River.
- 1.4 Turn right (south) at stoplight onto Texas 173.
- 1.7 Turn left onto Riverhills Blvd. and begin a long climb through a residential neighborhood.
- 2.8 Turn left (south) onto Texas 16, carefully crossing lanes of traffic.
- 6.3 Turn left onto West Creek Rd.
- 7.0 Turn left (east) onto FM 2771.
- 11.6 Turn right (south) onto Texas 173 (faster traffic and more challenging terrain).
- 16.8 Turn left at the Camp Verde General Store. There is a nice picnic area on Verde Creek here. Follow the unmarked lane in front of the store for 1 mile.
- 17.8 Turn left onto FM 480. The animals at the Verde Valley Ranch at this intersection are llamas. There are several nice crossings of Verde Creek on this stretch.
- 22.1 Pass Center Point town sign.
- 22.7 Pass convenience store. FM 480 is also called San Antonio St. through town.
- 23.0 Turn left onto Skyline Dr.
- 23.1 Turn right onto Park St. and cross near a spillway on the Guadalupe River.
- 23.3 After the spillway, Park St. bends to the right where it meets River Rd. (unmarked). Stay straight on River Rd.
- 26.0 After some rough pavement over a creek crossing, enter a large apple orchard.
- 26.9 At Y intersection, bear right onto Wharton Rd.
- 29.0 Turn right onto Texas 173; be mindful of increased traffic.
- 31.8 After passing Kerrville-Schreiner State Park, turn right (north) onto Loop 534 at traffic light.
- 32.2 Turn left onto Texas 27 (also called Memorial Blvd.) at the traffic light; be mindful of high-speed traffic.
- 33.2 Finish at Schreiner College.

5

The Sawickis' Favorite Hill Country Challenge

Fredericksburg—Cherry Springs—
Crabapple Community—Fredericksburg

The town of Fredericksburg provides a perfect home base for bicycle touring, with sweet cycling in every direction. The summer climate is moderated by Hill Country elevations, the area's country roads are well maintained and lightly traveled, and rolling hills provide a variety of vistas and challenging terrain.

Fredericksburg is steeped in history, with many of its residents and much of its architecture reflective of its German heritage. Some of this history is preserved in interesting local museums and seasonal festivals. Restored buildings found throughout the downtown area house a variety of antiques shops, German bakeries, and handiwork stores to keep shoppers busy.

Carl and Sara Sawicki recently moved their business and their ten bikes to Fredericksburg to be in the middle of this colorful countryside. The Sawickis may ride as many as 10,000 miles in a year, and they have taken their cycling friends along most of the area's back roads. This route is the one they ride most often.

The ride heads north and west from Fredericksburg through pleasant ranch country and briefly across the divide between the Edwards Plateau and the Llano uplift. Before long you'll begin to climb back into the hills of the Edwards Plateau toward views of Enchanted Rock, one of the most unique and popular geological formations in Texas. The pink granite of Enchanted Rock has a measured age of one billion years and is among the oldest exposed rocks in North America. Enchanted Rock State Park is worth a separate trip for some special hiking or picnicking.

The ride continues along Crabapple Creek through the Crabapple community, an early farming settlement established after the founding of Fredericksburg in the mid-nineteenth century. After some more climbing and rewarding views into the Hill Country, you return to downtown Fredericksburg.

Throughout this ride you'll be surrounded by all the variety of wildlife, vegetation, and scenery that the Texas Hill Country contains. Wildflowers in the spring and white-tailed deer in the fall are special attractions. Remember that you are likely to encounter loose livestock on some of these country roads at all times during the year. Also, expect numerous cattle-guard crossings.

Fredericksburg is populated with charming bed-and-breakfasts and with Sunday houses, which are tiny homes originally built by area farmers who traveled to town for market on Saturdays or church on Sundays. The chamber of commerce or local bed-and-breakfast association can help you arrange a stay. A wide range of food and atmosphere can be found in many quality restaurants, where the German specialties are especially appealing to hungry cyclists after a long ride.

The Basics

Start: In Fredericksburg behind the Gillespie County courthouse, on the corner of Main St. (US 290) and Adams St. (Texas 16).
Distance: 53.5 miles.
Terrain: Rolling hills with three challenging climbs.
Roads: Mostly on quiet, low-traffic country roads. US 290 (used for 3.0 miles), Texas 16 (used for 1.5 miles), and RM 965 (used for 0.7 mile) have some faster traffic, especially on weekends, but there is ample lane space and shoulder to accommodate cyclists.
Food: Plenty of options in Fredericksburg, but no convenience stores along the route. This tour is for cyclists who are comfortable traveling with their own provisions and spare parts.

Miles & Directions

- 0.0 Exit courthouse parking lot to the west by turning left off the Nimitz Pkwy. onto S. Crockett St.
- 0.1 Turn right at stop sign onto W. San Antonio St.
- 0.6 Turn left onto Bowie St.
- 1.7 Turn left at stop sign onto US 290; be mindful of increased traffic.
- 4.6 Turn right onto Loudon Rd. You'll cross at least seven cattle guards in the next 7 miles on this road, as well as seasonal low-water crossings. *Always walk these low-water crossings, even though they may look shallow.*
- 11.8 Turn right onto Pecan Creek Rd. You'll cross four cattle guards in the next 1.8 miles on this road.
- 13.4 Turn left onto Old Mason Rd.
- 13.9 Cross cattle guard and turn left onto US 87; be mindful of faster traffic.
- 15.9 Pass the Hilltop Café on your left.
- 19.3 Begin a descent, with an outstanding view of the beginning of the Llano Basin from the Edwards Plateau. At mile 20.1 on the right is a highway rest stop (no facilities). Note historical marker about early settler John Meusebach.
- 23.6 After entering the Cherry Springs community, turn right onto Cherry Springs Rd. You'll cross four cattle guards and several seasonal low-water crossings on this road.
- 26.7 Turn left briefly onto RM 2323.
- 26.9 Quick right turn onto Keese-Sagebiel Rd. You'll cross eight cattle guards in the next 4 miles. As you climb, your first views of Enchanted Rock will appear in the distance straight ahead when your reach mile 29.1.
- 30.9 Turn right onto Keese Rd. There will be three cattle guards to cross in the next mile.
- 32.0 Turn left onto Welgehausen. The next 4-mile stretch affords some excellent views of Enchanted Rock. Be mindful of loose livestock on this stretch of road, as well as seven cattle guards.
- 34.9 Beginning of a steep 0.5-mile climb.

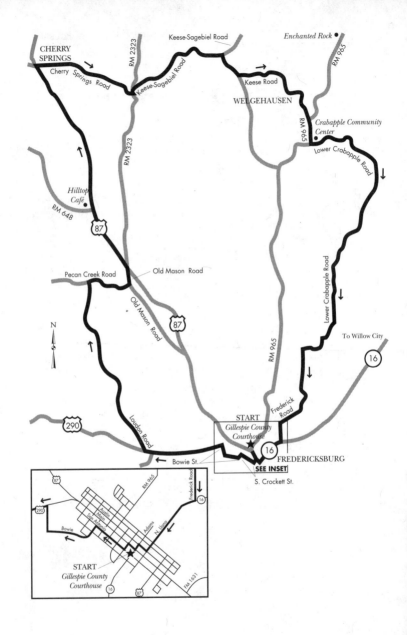

CHERRY
SPRINGS

Cherry Springs Road

RM 2323

Keese-Sagebiel Road

Keese-Sagebiel Road

Keese Road

Enchanted Rock ●

RM 965

WELGEHAUSEN

*Crabapple Community
Center*

Lower Crabapple Road

RM 2323

*Hilltop
Café* ●

RM 648

87

Pecan Creek Road

Old Mason Road

Old Mason Road

87

Lower Crabapple Road

RM 965

N

To Willow City

16

Loudan Road

290

Frederick Road

START
*Gillespie County
Courthouse* ★

16

FREDERICKSBURG

← Bowie St.

SEE INSET

S. Crockett St.

87

RM 965

Frederick Road

290

Bowie

Austin
Main
San Antonio

Adams

N. Llano

16

Adams

FM 1631

START
*Gillespie County
Courthouse*

16

87

- 36.1 Turn right onto RM 965; be mindful of faster traffic.
- 36.8 Turn left onto Lower Crabapple Rd. There are two left-hand turns close together here—be sure to take the second, which puts you onto the paved road and over the first of seven cattle guards during the next 3.2 miles.
- 36.9 Bear left over a cattle guard at the T intersection. This is still Lower Crabapple Rd. You will pass the Crabapple Community Center in 0.3 mile.
- 40.0 Continue straight on Lower Crabapple Rd. past the intersection with Eckert Rd. The next cattle guard at the entrance of Shooting Star Ranch is the first of ten you will encounter during the next 10.8 miles.
- 42.8 Be prepared for a steep climb over the next 0.3 mile. Your reward will be a long, gradual descent.
- 49.5 Another steep climb, this time for 0.7 mile. Your reward here will be some excellent Hill Country views.
- 50.9 Turn left onto Frederick Rd., a wide neighborhood street.
- 51.7 Turn right onto N. Llano, which is also Texas 16. Be mindful of increased traffic speeds.
- 53.2 Turn right at traffic light onto Austin St.
- 53.3 Turn left at stop sign onto Adams St.
- 53.5 Cross Main St. and finish behind Gillespie County courthouse.

6

Willow City Ramble

Willow City Loop

The Willow City Loop is a Hill Country gem on display just a few miles north of Fredericksburg. Tucked away between the Edwards Plateau and the Llano uplift near Enchanted Rock, this route winds its way through some of the oldest and most unique geology in central Texas.

The crown jewel of this route is the beautiful country of the first thirteen miles as seen from a narrow roadway winding downward through the canyons carved by Coal Creek. The setting is extraordinary, amid fields thick with mesquite, pecan, and live oak trees and carpeted with a dazzling array of wildflowers each spring. The Willow City Loop is home to all manner of Texas wildlife, with a special abundance of white-tailed deer.

As with many rural routes that traverse private property, cattle guards are employed to control livestock, and there are many to cross along the Willow City Loop. As you ride, be mindful that cattle, deer, sheep, and other animals may be sharing the road with you. There are several creek bed crossings as well, most of which are dry, but all of which may fill up seasonally depending on rainfall.

After leaving the Willow City Loop, your ride will be largely uphill on Texas 16. There are some wonderful vistas behind you, and riding this route in the opposite direction allows for a more relaxed view of Mount Nebo and Bell Mountain in the distance. The Willow City Loop is so rich in scenery that following this course in the opposite direction will seem like a completely different ride.

You'll also pass the Bell Mountain Vineyards on Texas 16 before returning to Willow City. Begun some twenty years ago, these vineyards established the first appellation (a federally recognized grape-growing area) in Texas. There is a tasting room and complimentary tours, but be sure to call ahead for times and an appointment if you plan a visit.

The Willow City community is quite small, and Willow City itself is nothing more than an intersection. There are no stores here, so be sure to bring whatever you need with you. You should be able to find places to park near the small utility building at the start or along the curbside of RM 1323. There are also some highway parking spots back on Texas 16.

Willow City attracts large numbers of sightseers during the spring wildflower season and avid sportsmen during the autumn hunting season. Wildflower watchers bring lots of slow-moving traffic to the route during spring weekends and holidays. Hunters bring guns in the fall. Be mindful of their presence if you choose to visit during these times of the year.

Be mindful, too, of the signs at the entrance to the Willow City Loop reminding visitors that the land through which the road passes is private property. Much of this wild and beautiful course is unfenced, and it is easy to forget that you are passing by people's homes. Respect for private property goes a long way toward making friends in rural Texas.

The Basics

Start: Willow City at the intersection of RM 1323 and the Willow City Loop. Take Texas 16 north from Fredericksburg (about 14 miles) and turn right on RM 1323.

Length: 21.3 miles.

Terrain: Rolling hills with some significant climbing on Texas 16.

Roads: The Willow City Loop is a narrow country road that is lightly traveled except during the spring wildflower season, when it is very busy. Texas 16 has higher-speed traffic but ample lane and shoulder space to accommodate bikes. RM 1323 is also lightly trav-

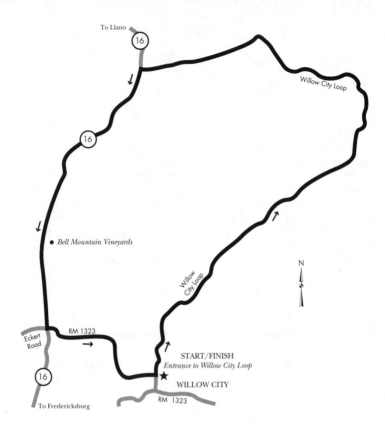

To Llano

16

Willow City Loop

16

● Bell Mountain Vineyards

N

Willow City Loop

Eckert Road

RM 1323

16

To Fredericksburg

START/FINISH
Entrance to Willow City Loop

★

WILLOW CITY

RM 1323

eled. Road surfaces are generally well maintained, although portions of the Willow City Loop may be rough.

Food: Bring what you need with you.

Miles & Directions

■   0.0 The Willow City Loop begins at the intersection with RM 1323.

There will be twenty-one cattle guards to cross before you reach Texas 16, along with several seasonal low-water crossings.

■   3.9 Steep descent of 0.5 miles begins—enjoy the view.
■   9.0 With interesting rock outcroppings in the distance, begin to climb out of the valley.
■   13.0 Exit the Willow City Loop by turning left onto Texas 16; be mindful of faster traffic. Texas 16 is generally uphill, and there are nice views behind you as you climb.
■   17.8 Pass Bell Mountain Vineyards on the left, and Old Eckert Cemetery on the right (mile 18.1), and Eckert Rd. on the right (mile 18.5).
■   18.6 Turn left off Texas 16 onto RM 1323.
■   21.3 Finish in Willow City.

7

Luckenbach Cruise

Fredericksburg—Luckenbach—Fredericksburg

Tiny Luckenbach is as much an event as it is a location. Hidden away off a side road in the countryside southeast of Fredericksburg, Luckenbach can be hard to find and harder to forget. The general store, post office, and dance hall that make up Luckenbach are full of unique charm and interesting characters. Among other things, Luckenbach is renowned for impromptu country music performances and an eclectic country manner. If you stop there, be careful not to get so relaxed that you can't get back on your bike and finish the ride.

The route to Luckenbach starts in Fredericksburg at the Gillespie County courthouse and heads south out of town toward the Pedernales River. Once off the main road, you'll have a pleasant ride along the river for a while, past rams and sheep grazing in nicely kept fields.

As the route continues east onto Meusebach Road, it enters land first settled in the mid-nineteenth century by German immigrants fleeing social and political unrest in Europe. Thousands of German families, under the banner of the Society for the Protection of German Immigrants in Texas, acquired a large land grant in the Hill Country from the Republic of Texas. Unbeknownst to the society at the time, this land was Indian country, full of hostile Apache and Comanche.

Meusebach Road is named for John Meusebach, the society's leader. Meusebach was able to negotiate a treaty with these Indians, organize his impoverished followers, and settle these lands.

Meusebach is acclaimed as the only man to have signed a lasting treaty of peace with any Indian tribe in Texas.

Past the Meusebach Road, the course enters quiet communities that were once commercial centers for the farms and ranches of the Pedernales and Blanco valleys. Little more than road signs now remain of Cain City and Grapetown, whose fortunes came with the construction of a railroad just before World War I and went with its abandonment just before World War II. Historically, these were important crossroads by which the Hill Country was connected with San Antonio. Today they are tiny rural communities with rustic bed-and-breakfasts tucked away along side roads.

After leaving Luckenbach, the ride returns to Fredericksburg through some lovely pecan groves and farmland. A shorter option starting in Luckenbach is included; it avoids the roads with heavier traffic featured on the full tour and allows a more leisurely visit in Luckenbach before or after your ride.

The Basics

Start: In Fredericksburg at the Gillespie County courthouse. Mileage is marked from the corner of Nimitz Pkwy. (behind the courthouse) and Texas 16, which is called Adams St. in town.
Miles: 37.2 miles or 13.2 miles starting from Luckenbach.
Terrain: Rolling hills; no extraordinary climbs.
Roads: Some riding on busy roads: Texas 16 (used for 4.8 miles), US 87 (used for 1.3 miles), and US 290 (used for 1.1 miles) all have four lanes; there are shoulders on Texas 16 and US 290. Some traffic on RM 1376, otherwise isolated country roads.
Food: Lots of choices in Fredericksburg; the Luckenbach general store/post office (closed Wednesdays).

Miles & Directions

■   0.0 Begin by exiting the courthouse and turning right (south) onto Texas 16/Adams St., which is four lanes and provides an adequate shoulder after 0.3 miles.

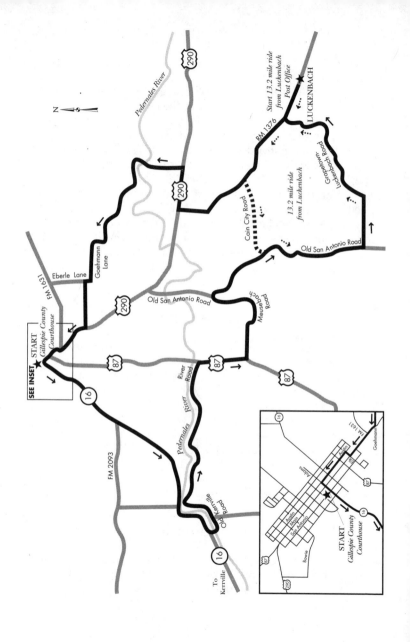

- 3.3 Pass entrance to Lady Bird Johnson Municipal Park on the right.
- 4.8 Carefully turn left across traffic onto the Old Kerrville Rd., a narrow country road with little traffic.
- 5.0 Turn left onto River Rd. You'll cross ten cattle guards in the next 4 miles on this secluded road.
- 6.6 Continue straight past the unmarked road to the left.
- 7.8 Take special care crossing the cattle guard here, which is usually in poor repair.
- 8.7 At the stop sign, turn right at the T intersection with US 87; be mindful of narrow or nonexistent shoulder and faster traffic (four lanes).
- 10.0 Pass the Meusebach Country Store on the left, which is open seasonally to sell peaches and produce.
- 10.2 Carefully turn left across traffic onto Meusebach Rd. There will be eight cattle guards, some nice vistas, and maybe a road-runner or two along this road for the next 3 miles.
- 13.1 At unmarked Y intersection, bear right onto the Old San Antonio Rd.
- 15.3 Continue right on the Old San Antonio Rd. past the turn marked with a sign for the Cain City Cottage B & B on the left.
- 17.7 Turn left onto Grapetown-Luckenbach Rd. Enjoy a nice river crossing at mile 20.0.
- 22.5 At the stop sign T intersection, turn right onto RM 1376 (unmarked).
- 22.8 The next right is unmarked, at a 45-degree angle to RM 1376 and with a stop sign in the other direction. Turn right onto this road and ride into Luckenbach.

This turn comes up quickly and is easy to miss. If you do pass this turn, the next right in 0.4 mile, just before a bridge crossing, also will take you into Luckenbach.

- 23.2 Arrive at the Luckenbach post office, closed Wednesdays.
- 23.4 After passing the post office and the dance hall, continue out of Luckenbach and turn left at the stop sign onto RM 1376. Continue past the Old Luckenbach Rd. immediately to the right.

- 23.9 Pass the Grapetown Rd. intersection on the left.
- 26.0 Pass Cain City Rd. on the left.
- 28.0 At stop sign and T intersection of US 290—KOA campgrounds on the right—turn right onto US 290. It has four lanes, faster traffic, and a slight shoulder.
- 29.1 Carefully turn left across traffic onto Goehmann La., immediately crossing the first of six cattle guards in the next 6 miles.
- 34.3 Stay on Goehmann La. by bearing hard left at an unmarked intersection with Eberle La.
- 35.6 At the stoplight intersection with Main St. (US 290 becomes Main St. in town), turn right. Note faster traffic; there are four lanes with no marked shoulder but extra lane space sufficient to accommodate bikes.
- 36.2 The bridge over Barron's Creek has some cracks in the road near the curb, making for a rough ride.
- 36.5 Turn right onto Elk St. to get away from Main St. traffic.
- 36.6 Go 1 block and turn left at stop sign onto Austin St.—Nimitz Historical Park is on this corner.
- 37.1 At the stop sign on Adams St. turn left; pass the chamber of commerce.
- 37.2 Continue straight through the stoplight at Main St. and finish at the Gillespie County courthouse on the left.

Shorter Option Starting in Luckenbach

- 0.0 Leave Luckenbach from the back (north), past the parking area and up the small hill.
- 0.4 Turn left onto RM 1376 (unmarked).
- 0.7 Pass Grapetown Rd. to the left.
- 2.9 Turn left onto the Cain City Rd.
- 5.0 Turn left onto the Old San Antonio Rd. (unmarked).
- 5.3 Continue right on the Old San Antonio Rd. past the turn marked with a sign for the Cain City Cottage B & B on the left.
- 7.7 Turn left onto the Grapetown-Luckenbach Rd. Enjoy a nice river crossing at mile 10.0.

- 12.5 At the stop sign T intersection, turn right onto RM 1376 (unmarked).
- 12.8 The next right is unmarked, at a 45-degree angle to RM 1376 and with a stop sign in the other direction. Turn right onto this road into Luckenbach.
- 13.2 Finish at the Luckenbach post office.

8

LBJ Country Cruise

LBJ Parks—Stonewall—Cave Creek—
Albert—LBJ Parks

Much has been written about the influence the land of the Pedernales River Valley has had in shaping the character and life of Lyndon B. Johnson. This tour takes you through the land surrounding his family ranch, which served as his "western White House" during his presidency.

The National Park Service administers the LBJ ranch itself, which is still used by the Johnson family. The state park across the river from the ranch includes a visitors center and serves as the starting point for bus tours of the ranch and for this beautiful bike ride.

Most of this ride follows seldom-traveled one-lane roads through farmland and ranch country. Because these lanes are so isolated from traffic and development, the white-tailed deer that populate the area are especially visible. If you try this route anytime in late fall or early winter, expect to see deer jump a fence and cross your path, especially along Cave Creek Road or the Lower Albert Road.

After leaving the state park, you'll ride briefly along the shore of the Pedernales River toward the town of Stonewall. In late spring and early summer, roadside stands spring up to sell the wonderfully sweet, juicy peaches Stonewall is famous for. The ride then heads north and west (and uphill) along two ranch roads toward the secluded country lanes that give this tour its special character. A shorter option turns south and passes through the farmland of the Albert community. The full tour turns north through hillier ranch land with some terrific views and then returns through the Cave Creek community.

The finish along RM 1 is special as well. This stretch borders the Pedernales River, passes a lovely church and a field full of buffalo at the Sauer-Beckmann Living History Farm (on the grounds of the state historical park), and finishes across the river from the presidential gravesite. After your ride, you might enjoy the exhibits at the park headquarters or the bus tour of the LBJ ranch.

The Basics

Start: LBJ State Park, at the intersection of Park Rd. 52 and RM 1. There is parking at the visitors center, which is located on US 290, 65 miles west of Austin and 15 miles east of Fredericksburg.

Distance: 36.5 miles or 21.7 miles.

Terrain: Some climbing on the RM roads and on Klein-Ahrens Rd.

Roads: The RM roads are two lanes without shoulders and are lightly traveled. The country lanes are narrow, well paved, and almost devoid of traffic.

Food: Vending machines at park headquarters; convenience store across US 290 at the park entrance.

Miles & Directions

- 0.0 Exit LBJ State Park from Park Rd. 52 by turning left (west) onto RM 1, which runs parallel to the Pedernales River.
- 2.0 Turn right (north) on RM 1623 and cross river. Two lanes, no shoulder, little traffic.
- 5.0 At stop sign, turn left (west) onto RM 2721. Two lanes, no shoulder.
- 6.8 Turn right onto Klein-Ahrens Rd., a secluded path with some terrific vistas and challenging hills. There will be seven cattle guard crossings in the next 5 miles. Lots of cedar, Spanish live oaks, and mesquite trees shade portions of this path.

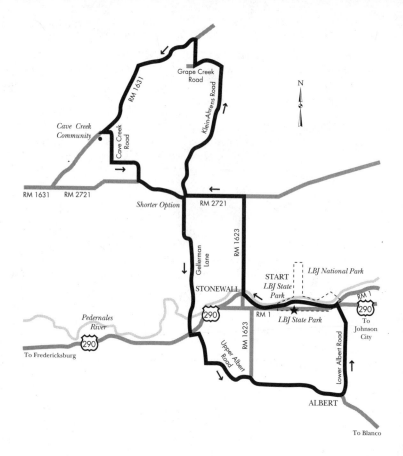

For a shorter option totaling 21.7 miles, turn left here onto Gellerman La. and follow directions for the full tour from mile 21.6 to return to the LBJ Parks.

- 12.1 Bear right at the unmarked intersection. This is Grape Creek Rd. (Continuing straight is a dead end in 0.3 mile.)
- 12.9 At T intersection, turn left onto the unmarked road, which is RM 1631.
- 17.5 After entering the community of Cave Creek and passing the St. Paul Lutheran Church, make a hard left turn onto Cave Creek Rd.
- 20.0 At T intersection, turn left at the stop sign onto RM 2721, which is unmarked here.
- 21.6 Turn right onto Gellerman La., immediately up a short climb. Road is one lane and secluded through farmland and ranch land, with some low-water crossings. The shorter option continues from here.
- 26.1 At stop sign, road intersects with US 290. Cross carefully and bear immediately left onto the Upper Albert Rd. at its intersection with Hahn Rd. (Hahn Rd. is a dead end.)
- 26.4 Stay on the Upper Albert Rd. by bearing right at Y intersection.
- 29.1 At stop sign, turn right onto RM 1623 (unmarked).
- 32.3 After entering the community of Albert, turn left onto the Lower Albert Rd.
- 35.2 At stop sign, Lower Albert Rd. intersects with US 290. Cross carefully and continue straight, past church playground on the left.
- 35.4 At the stop sign, turn left onto RM 1, past the Trinity Lutheran Church.
- 36.4 LBJ Ranch and gravesite are visible across the river.
- 36.5 Finish at entrance to the LBJ State Park.

9

Two Gruene/River Road Cruises

Gruene—River Road—Sattler—Gruene

The common thread tying these two tours from Gruene together is the extraordinary ten-mile portion of River Road paralleling the Guadalupe River. It's downhill for most of the way along River Road, and four wide river crossings provide terrific views. Along the river several well-known rapids with colorfully named passages like Slumber Falls and Hueco Springs provide serious challenges to rafters and pleasant scenery for cyclists. Large portions of River Road follow a narrow passage between the tree-shaded river on one side and limestone cliffs on the other.

During the summer, this stretch of the Guadalupe River is very popular with swimmers and campers. Consequently, the road is jammed with seasonal businesses renting equipment and serving food along its course. During the rest of the year, however, this stretch seems abandoned, as the seasonal businesses are boarded up and the roads are emptied of traffic. As a result, a ride along River Road is glorious anytime after Labor Day and before Memorial Day.

These Cruises start in front of Gruene Hall, which may be one of the oldest dance halls still in use in Texas. It's a fine place to relax and listen to some music before or after a bike ride. The small community of Gruene, named after an early settler, was established in the 1850s around cotton farming. Largely neglected after the Depression, Gruene was restored in the 1970s as a recreation and tourist destination. Rafting and tubing on the Guadalupe River, country music at Gruene Hall, and a variety of restaurants are some of the principal attractions.

Both of the biking options offered here begin with the same route down River Road. At the end of River Road is the town of Sattler. The first option continues straight to the Canyon Lake Dam. A short side trip up the access road to the top of the dam affords a magnificent view of the lake. The route loops back on FM 306, with a good climb on the way back to Gruene.

The second option turns left at Sattler and follows busier FM roads with wide shoulders toward New Braunfels. These roads are dramatically different from River Road; they pass through open country and are generally uphill. Near New Braunfels, the route turns north and reenters quieter, sheltered roads along the Hueco Springs Loop before returning to Gruene.

The Basics

Start: At Gruene Hall. Gruene is 2 miles west of I-35 (exit 191), about 45 miles north of San Antonio, and 45 miles south of Austin. Park in the large public lot across from Gruene Hall.
Length: Option one (north toward Canyon Lake Dam) is 30.7 miles. Option two (south toward New Braunfels) is 34.9 miles.
Terrain: Gently rolling hills—mostly downhill along River Rd. and generally uphill on the return, with a difficult 1-mile climb on each route.
Roads: River Rd. is two lanes with no shoulder. Traffic volume is *extremely* heavy on summer weekends and holidays, but very light from September to May. FM roads are two to four lanes with wide shoulders and higher-speed traffic.
Food: Several restaurants in Gruene; restaurants and convenience stores in Sattler. Stores along River Rd. are open only during the summer season.

Miles & Directions

- 0.0 Begin at Gruene Hall, at the end of Hunter Rd. Facing Gruene Hall, head down Gruene Rd. to the right.

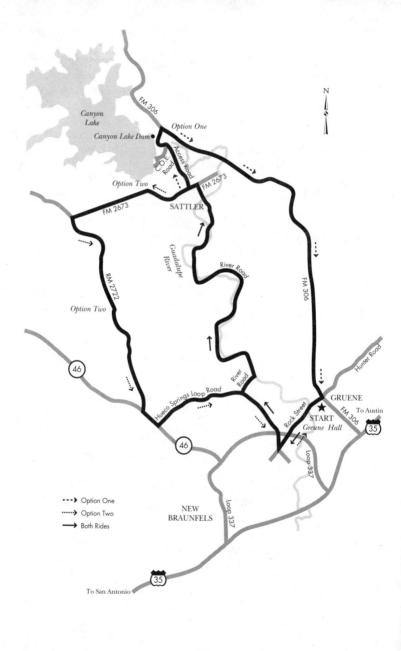

Canyon
Lake

FM 306

Option One

Canyon Lake Dam

C.O.E. Road

Access Road

Option Two

FM 2673

SATTLER

FM 2673

N

Guadalupe River

River Road

RM 2722

Option Two

FM 306

46

River Road

River Road

Hueco Springs Loop Road

Hunter Road

GRUENE

Rock Street

START
Greune Hall

FM 306

To Austin

35

46

Loop 337

NEW
BRAUNFELS

Loop 337

- - -▶ Option One
······▶ Option Two
——▶ Both Rides

35

To San Antonio

- 0.2 Gruene Rd. turns sharply to the left and then descends quickly as you cross the Guadalupe River. This is a popular crossing for tube rentals, so be mindful of pedestrians in the road here.
- 0.9 Bear right onto Rock St. at the Y intersection in the road.
- 1.6 At the end of Rock St., turn right at the stop sign onto River Rd.
- 1.9 Pass through the intersection of Loop 337 at the traffic light. A convenience store is on your right.
- 3.7 Bear right on River Rd. at its intersection with Hueco Springs Loop.

The next 10 miles wind along and across the Guadalupe River, past campgrounds and riverbanks shaded by cypress and live oak trees. Cliffs and vegetation come right up to the roadside in some stretches. A variety of Indian tribes once camped on the banks; a number of private campgrounds are now maintained for visitors. This stretch is especially attractive in early November when the foliage changes color. Be respectful of private property along this unique stretch.

- 5.2 First of four crossings, over wide bridges, of the Guadalupe River; excellent river views.
- 7.2 Second river crossing.
- 10.2 Third river crossing.
- 14.2 Fourth river crossing.
- 14.9 Caution-light intersection with FM 2673 in Sattler.

Option One (north toward Canyon Lake Dam)

- 14.9 At caution-light intersection with FM 2673 in Sattler, continue straight onto South Access Rd., beginning a steady climb.

You can shorten this option by 3.4 miles by turning right (east) onto FM 2673. After 1.5 miles, turn right onto FM 306 at the stoplight, and follow the directions for this option from mile 19.8 to return to Gruene.

- 16.8 Pass entrance to Canyon Lake Dam, C.O.E. road to the left. Follow South Access as it bends to the right at the base of the dam.

  The view of Canyon Lake from the top of the dam is worth the climb of the C.O.E. road. Turn left and after 0.5 mile you'll top the climb at a rest area with a great view. The entrance to a pedestrian walk (marked as the Vereda Real 5K Scenic Walk) across the dam is here. Riding to the end of the C.O.E. road and back adds 1.3 miles to this option.

- 17.4 Turn right (south) onto FM 306 at the stop sign T intersection. There's a center turn lane instead of a shoulder for 0.6 mile.
- 19.5 Cross Guadalupe River.
- 19.8 Pass intersection with FM 2673 to the right and immediately cross Guadalupe River again.
- 20.8 Begin a 1-mile climb over some more challenging terrain. FM 306 is less protected from sun and wind than River Rd.
- 27.9 Pass town sign for New Braunfels.
- 30.2 Turn right at the stoplight onto Hunter Rd.
- 30.7 Finish at Gruene Hall.

Option Two (south toward New Braunfels)

- 14.9 At caution-light intersection with FM 2673 in Sattler, turn left (west).
- 19.3 Turn left onto RM 2722 access road.
- 19.5 Continue through the stop sign (south) onto RM 2722, marked as the Texas Hill Country Trail. Wide shoulder continues.
- 22.2 Cross Bear Creek and begin steady climb for 1 mile.
- 27.0 At stop sign, carefully turn left (east) across traffic onto Texas 46 at the outskirts of New Braunfels. Wide shoulder continues.
- 27.8 Turn left onto Hueco Springs Loop Rd., a secluded country road.

- 31.1 Continue straight as Hueco Springs Loop Rd. merges with River Rd.
- 33.0 Continue straight through the stoplight intersection of River Rd. and Loop 337.
- 33.3 Turn left onto Rock St. Pass stop sign (mile 34.0) and continue onto Gruene Rd.
- 34.7 After crossing the river over rough pavement, the road grade increases sharply for a short climb back into Gruene.
- 34.9 Finish in front of Gruene Hall.

10

Devil's Backbone Cruise

Wimberley—Fischer—Wimberley

This is the first of two tours starting in Wimberley, a popular residential center near the edge of the Texas Hill Country. Early settler Pleasant Wimberley is the town's namesake, and even the chamber of commerce couldn't have picked a more apt name for its founding father.

This pleasant town is located in the Wimberley Valley along the confluence of the Blanco River and Cypress Creek. Over the last fifty years, the Wimberley Valley has become a favorite site for vacation and retirement homes. Tourism is a significant local industry, centered around outdoor recreation and shopping in interesting antiques and crafts stores.

All roads leaving the Wimberley Valley lead uphill. Luckily, the most forgiving route out of town is also the most peaceful route to cycle; it goes along the Fischer Store Road toward the "Devil's Backbone."

The Devil's Backbone is the nickname of an undulating stretch of Hill Country road near Canyon Lake between San Marcos and Wimberley. It is a favorite training ground for members of the nearby Southwest Texas State University cycling team. The Devil's Backbone features some steep climbing and long, gradual descents, along with excellent views into the surrounding Hill Country.

Leaving Wimberley the route follows a long, lovely passage along the Fischer Store Road. The ride through the Fischer community follows a tree-shaded road with a rough surface in places over creek crossings and past fields sheltering lots of wild game. Fischer was founded in the 1850s around the Fischer family dry-goods store, which at the time was housed in the metal building you'll pass at the end of the Fischer Store Road. The building now houses the Fischer post office, which had a Fischer family member as the postmaster from its opening in 1876 until 1993.

Leaving Fischer, the route turns east onto the Devil's Backbone. Be prepared for some climbing—and some great scenery—along this aptly named stretch of road. Your efforts will be rewarded with long views into the Wimberley Valley to the left and an occasional glimpse of Canyon Lake in the distance to the right.

By touring in the counterclockwise direction set out here, you'll descend, rather than climb, Spoke Hill on RM 12 on the way back to Wimberley. Spoke Hill got its name from early travelers who put logs through the spokes of their wagons and carts to control their slide down this steep hill. If you are tempted to test your endurance by riding this route in a clockwise direction, be mindful of the increased traffic, especially on weekends, along RM 12.

The Basics

Start: At Wimberley's "Old Town," at the intersection of RM 12 and Hays County Rd. 173. There's additional parking at the tourist information office 0.2 mile away.

Distance: 28.8 miles.

Terrain: Very hilly, with some challenging climbing along the Devil's Backbone and a steep descent of Spoke Hill.

Roads: RM 12 has moderate to heavy traffic, especially on weekends, and no shoulder. FM 32 has a wide shoulder for most of the course over the Devil's Backbone. The portion of the Fischer Store Rd. in Hays County has a rough surface. There is little traffic on the Fischer Store Rd.

Food: Lots of options in Wimberley; three stores along FM 32.

Miles & Directions

- 0.0 Head south on RM 12 from the intersection with County Rd. 173, across Cypress Creek.

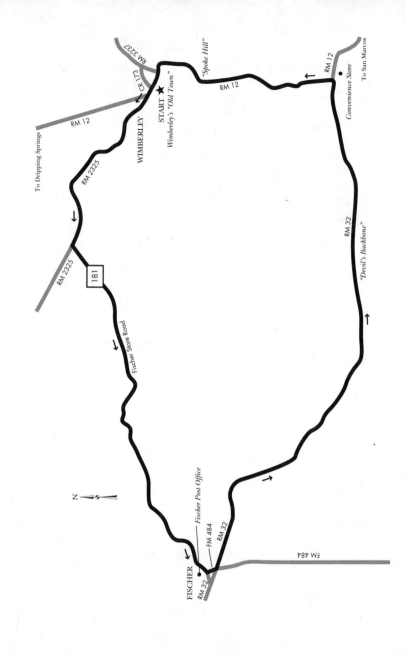

- 0.2 Continue straight through stoplight. Tourist information center is on the right.
- 0.6 Signs directing you to Blanco and RM 2325 to the left. There is no stoplight at this busy intersection. Turn left onto RM 2325, which has an improved shoulder in town.
- 4.2 Turn left onto Hays County Rd. 181, the Fischer Store Rd.
- 7.5 After a creek crossing, expect poor road conditions for the next 3 miles. At mile 9.9 cross a cattle guard, and at mile 11.9 pass the Fischer Bowling Club, a private club.
- 12.4 Stop sign at the intersection of Fischer Store Rd. and FM 484. Turn left (south) onto FM 484. The metal building to the right is the old Fischer Store.
- 12.6 At the stop sign intersection, turn left (east) onto FM 32. Shoulder is narrow at this point, and terrain becomes significantly more rolling.
- 17.0 Continue straight past the intersection with FM 3424. A wide shoulder appears. This is the heart of the Devil's Backbone. Be prepared for big hills and great views. A rest area on the left at mile 19.5 affords terrific vistas of surrounding Hill Country peaks and valleys.
- 20.6 Pass two places for something to eat and drink—Riley's and the Devil's Backbone Tavern. Wide shoulder ends here.
- 24.4 Turn left onto RM 12. A convenience store is near this intersection on the right. Traffic increases on RM 12.
- 26.0 Begin descent of Spoke Hill.
- 28.3 Cross Blanco River and continue straight on RM 12 past the intersection with RM 3237.
- 28.8 Finish tour at "Old Town" at the intersection of Hays County Rd. 173 and RM 12.

11

Wimberley Metric Century Classic

Wimberley—Dripping Springs—
Driftwood—Wimberley

The Balcones Escarpment separates the flat farmland of the Blackland Prairie from the Hill Country of the Edwards Plateau. Wimberley is located west of this divide, within easy reach of the roads
running north and south along the escarpment. This second of two
tours starting in Wimberley explores the Hill Country along the
eastern edge of the Edwards Plateau.

In spring and fall, several organized tours sponsored along these
roads are popular with those who enjoy the special challenge and
reward of cycling over Hill Country terrain. There are always different tour distances to choose from, as Maynard Hershon points out
so colorfully in his commentary "They're Just CALLED Centuries"
(see Appendix A at the end of this book). The route outlined here
covers approximately 100 kilometers, a "metric century." Finishing
a metric century in an organized tour is a popular goal and, especially on the roads around Wimberley, a significant accomplish-
ment.

The first four miles of this route follow the same path out of the
Wimberley Valley as the **Devil's Backbone Cruise.** Continuing on
a long stretch through rolling ranch land, the course turns east toward a huge hill looming menacingly in the distance. The climb of
this hill isn't as bad as it first looks, and you'll be more than amply

rewarded with a roll along the top of a long ridge. Leaving these hills, the road drops down to Hays County Road 190, a beautiful, shaded lane along Onion Creek.

Several of the roads on this route cross Onion Creek, one of the longest and prettiest creeks in central Texas. Dammed in several places, it appears wide and full in some stretches, narrow and trickling in others. Onion Creek, and the roads you'll ride along its banks, alternately cut through bluffs, past groves of trees, and through open ranch land.

Leaving Hays County Road 190, you'll encounter some traffic passing through the town of Dripping Springs. Unless you elect to shorten the ride by returning to Wimberley on heavily traveled RM 12, you'll soon be out in the country again on the way toward Camp Ben McCullough. The camp was organized one hundred years ago as a reunion site for Confederate war veterans; it is now a park and campgrounds. Across the street is the Salt Lick, a renowned barbeque restaurant.

Not far beyond the camp is the small community of Driftwood. After passing the residences and ranches of Driftwood, you'll find some more nice crossings of Onion Creek and a last chance for provisions at the Hays City Store. From the Hays City Store, you'll soon begin a long, gradual descent back into the Wimberley Valley to finish your ride.

The Basics

Start: In Wimberley's "Old Town," at the intersection of RM 12 and Hays County Rd. 173. There's additional parking at the tourist information office 0.2 mile away.

Length: 61.7 miles. There are two options to shorten the ride from Dripping Springs by using roads with heavier traffic.

Terrain: Rolling hills, with one big climb on RM 165.

Roads: Moderate to heavy traffic on the roads around Dripping Springs (RM 12, RM 150, and US 290). RM 3237 may have some traffic, especially on weekends. Otherwise, quiet country roads with light traffic.

Food: Several options in Wimberley and Dripping Springs; renowned barbeque at Salt Lick; Hays City Store.

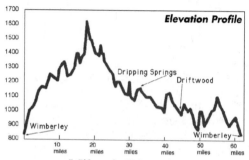

Miles & Directions

- 0.0 Head south from the intersection with Hays County Rd. 173 on RM 12, across Cypress Creek.
- 0.6 Signs directing you to Blanco and RM 2325 to the left. There is no stoplight at this busy intersection. Turn right onto RM 2325, which has an improved shoulder in town.
- 4.2 Continue straight on RM 2325 past intersection on left with Hays County Rd. 181, the Fischer Store Rd. Pass through rolling ranch land supporting sheep, goats, and cattle.
- 16.2 At stop sign, turn right (east) onto RM 165.
- 17.9 Nice views at top of climb.
- 24.1 Turn right on Hays County Rd. 190 as RM 165 bends to the left. (If you come to US 290, you've gone too far.) This is a lovely country road, narrow and shaded, that parallels and crosses Onion Creek for much of the way.
- 25.7 Continue straight on Hays County Rd. 190 past intersection with Hays County Rd. 198.
- 28.0 Continue straight on Hays County Rd. 190 past intersection with Hays County Rd. 189.
- 30.6 Go over low-water crossing, then turn left at the intersection with Hays County Rd. 220.
- 32.9 Turn right at the stop sign onto US 290. There is a shoulder and several opportunities for provisions in Dripping Springs.

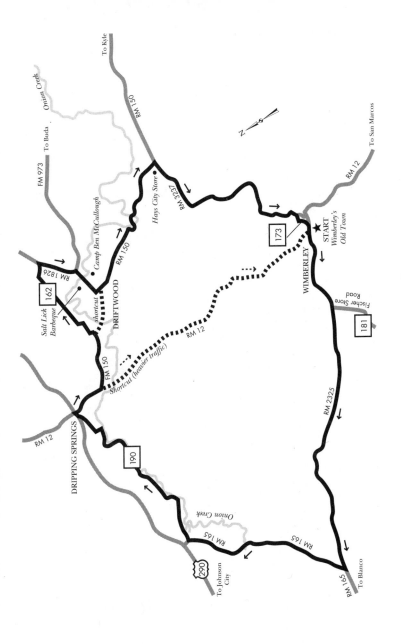

- 33.2 Turn right (south) onto RM 12. Shoulder disappears but traffic continues.
- 34.9 Turn left onto FM 150, also without a shoulder but moderate traffic.

To shorten the ride, continue straight on RM 12 for another 13 miles to return to Wimberley. This is a heavily traveled road with no shoulder.

- 37.6 Turn left off of FM 150 and then quickly left again onto Hays County Rd. 162, a secluded country road.

To shorten the ride by 5.2 miles, continue straight on FM 150 for another 2.5 miles and rejoin the full tour at mile 45.3 to return to Wimberley.

- 42.1 At stop sign, turn right (south) onto RM 1826.
- 43.9 Continue straight on RM 1826 past intersection to the left of FM 973.
- 44.1 Pass the Salt Lick restaurant on the right and Camp Ben McCullough on the left.
- 45.3 At stop sign, turn left (east) onto FM 150.
- 45.9 Pass through Driftwood.
- 48.9 First Onion Creek crossing.
- 49.2 Second Onion Creek crossing.
- 52.3 At stop sign, turn right (west) onto RM 3237, past the Hays City Store.
- 61.2 As RM 3237 bends left just past the Wimberley town sign, continue straight onto Hays County Rd. 173.
- 61.7 Finish your tour at "Old Town."

12

Lost Pines Cruise

Bastrop—Bastrop State Park—Buescher State Park— Smithville—Upton—Bastrop

The centerpiece of this ride is the secluded road through the pine forests of both Bastrop and Buescher State Parks. The work of the Civilian Conservation Corps here during the 1930s resulted in a special spot for campers, hikers, and now cyclists to enjoy.

The thick stands of loblolly pines preserved in these parks are located in the middle of otherwise flat and open farmland and ranch country. Pine trees were once found all across Texas, but geological and climatic changes over the ages altered land conditions so that these trees now thrive only in the "Piney Woods" to the east. Somehow an isolated pocket near Bastrop, where the parks are located, was left untouched, and some seventy square miles of pine forests remain here in central Texas.

Bastrop began as a Spanish fort along the Old San Antonio Road. The harvesting of lumber from the pine forests became a major industry, and Bastrop featured prominently in the history of the Republic of Texas and the early days of Texas statehood. A feel for these times remains in the restored homes, buildings, and churches that blanket Bastrop, more than one hundred of which are listed on the National Register of Historic Places. One of these interesting buildings, the Bastrop Opera House, is the beneficiary of the Tour de Bastrop, a bike race and tour held over Labor Day weekend along the roads described in this Cruise.

Many of the rural Texas roads that provide such pleasant cycling today began as simple cattle paths and wagon trails. The roads you'll travel from Bastrop are no exception. A display in front of the Bastrop County courthouse describes the path of the early Spanish "Royal Road" from Mexico to Florida (explored more closely on the **El Camino Real Challenge**) through Bastrop. A historical marker at the park entrance recounts the development of a trace to join Stephen F. Austin's early settlements further east (explored more closely on **Austin's Colony Cruise**) with Bastrop. Cycling along these pathways may provide some insight to and a connection with the efforts of these early travelers.

The ride through the pine forests is so pleasant that you may wish to simply turn around and retrace your steps once you reach the end of the park roads. The roads through the parks are quite hilly, in marked contrast to the surrounding countryside. The full tour exits the parks and enters Smithville, which began as a trading post and ferry point across the Colorado River. Continuing past Smithville and back to Bastrop through the ranch country and farmland south of the parks will give you a feel for how "lost" the Lost Pines really are.

The Basics

Start: At the Bastrop County courthouse. Bastrop is located 30 miles southeast of Austin on Texas 71. There is public parking around the courthouse.

Length: 37.2 miles. Riding out and back on the park roads is 30.8 miles.

Terrain: Very hilly through the state parks; otherwise fairly flat through open farmland and ranch land.

Roads: Narrow park roads are extremely isolated. FM roads are lightly traveled. Higher-speed traffic on Texas 95 (used for 1.9 miles) and Texas 71 (used for 1.7 miles). There is a left turn across busy traffic at a stoplight intersection on Texas 71.

Food: Restaurants and stores in Bastrop; soda machines at both park headquarters; stores in Smithville.

Miles & Directions

- 0.0 From the Bastrop County courthouse, at the corner of Pine St. and Pecan St., turn left onto Pecan St. Continue straight on Pecan for a short warm-up through town.
- 0.5 Turn right onto Cedar.
- 1.1 Turn right at stop sign onto Texas 95.
- 1.5 Turn left (east) through the four-way stop onto Loop 150/ Texas 21, following the sign directing you to the Bastrop State Park. Begin a short climb.
- 2.2 At the top of hill, Loop 150 and Texas 21 diverge. Stay to the right on Loop 150.
- 2.4 At the intersection of American Legion Dr. and Loop 150, a sign directs you to the entrance of the Bastrop State Park, which is visible to the left. Turn left then immediately right into the park onto Park Rd. 1A.
- 2.8 Pass park headquarters.
- 3.1 Park Rd. 1A splits in two. Both directions eventually lead to the Park Rd. 1C intersection. Take the left—it's a mile shorter and not as hilly.
- 3.6 Turn right and stay on Park Rd. 1A at the intersection with Park Rd. 1B. Pass a small lake and begin climbing.
- 4.2 At top of climb, turn left onto Park Rd. 1C, following the sign directing you to Buescher State Park. There are four cattle guards to cross in the next 4 miles.
- 13.5 Continue straight on Park Rd. 1C past the unmarked Y intersection with County Rd. 174 to the right.
- 14.5 Turn right and stay on Park Rd. 1C at the intersection with Park Rd. 1E.
- 15.4 Pass Buescher State Park headquarters.

For a shorter option totaling 30.8 miles, turn around here and retrace your path back to Bastrop. Consider slight variations on the way back by staying straight on Park Rd. 1A at its intersection with Park Rd. 1C or by continuing straight on Chestnut St. toward downtown Bastrop at the intersection of Texas 95 and Texas 21.

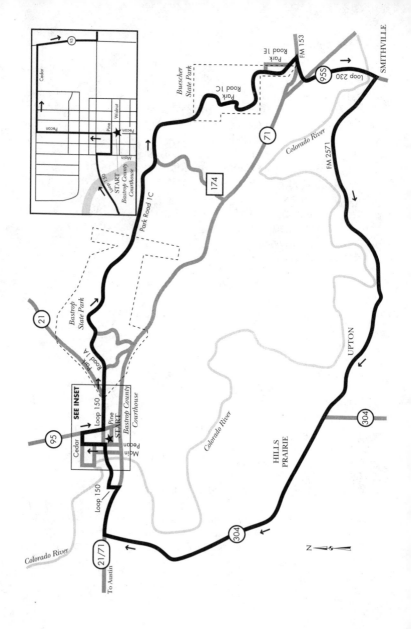

- 15.5 At the stop sign, turn right onto Texas 71, mindful of higher-speed traffic.
- 15.9 Continue straight under the highway underpass onto Texas 95 South/Loop 230 East toward Smithville, marked as the Texas Independence Trail.
- 17.6 After entering Smithville, cross the Colorado River.
- 17.8 Turn right (west) onto FM 2571 toward Upton, passing through open ranch land.
- 24.6 Cross railroad tracks set at a slanting angle to the road (be sure to cross them perpendicularly) and enter community of Upton.
- 27.6 At stop sign, turn right (north) on Texas 304. Traffic increases.
- 30.0 Pass Hill's Prairie Grocery on the right.
- 34.9 Turn right (east) onto Texas 21/Texas 71, with higher-speed traffic and a wide shoulder.
- 36.2 Use caution turning left at second stoplight onto Loop 150 East, where sign directs you to the historical district.
- 36.5 Use cement hike and bike path to cross the Colorado River over the Iron Bridge, which was constructed in 1922.
- 36.9 Turn right onto Main St.
- 37.0 Turn left onto Pine St.
- 37.2 Finish at the Bastrop County courthouse.

13

Pflugerville Farm Country Challenge

Pflugerville—Cele—Coupland—Manda—
New Sweden—Richland—Pflugerville

Pflugerville sits on the eastern edge of the Balcones Escarpment, the dividing line between the rich farmland of the Blackland Prairies to the east and the Hill Country of the Edwards Plateau to the west. The relatively flat character of the landscape and the country roads free of traffic make this area a favorite for both pleasure rides and early season training for serious cyclists.

Pflugerville was once a small farming and ranching community, established by German ranchers who were joined later by Mexicans displaced by the 1910 revolution. The residential and commercial development transforming the rural communities along the I–35 corridor is rapidly altering the character of Pflugerville, which is now a residential suburb of Austin to the south and Round Rock to the north.

The wonderful farmland to the east remains unaffected by this development and retains much of its original charm and special character. The area has changed little since its settlement, and over the years cyclists have passed several movie shoots that used this rural setting as a backdrop to re-create the feel of country life in years past.

The character of the countryside changes with the cycles of crops growing in the fields, and taking a ride in the warm evenings of late summer, when flocks of birds hover over the harvests, is especially enjoyable. Other than farm equipment at harvest time, area roads are lightly traveled as they pass through open countryside containing horse stables, cattle pastures, and fertile fields.

Three loops starting in the Pflugerville town park are set out here. Each loop extends a little further to the east. The two longer loops pass the lovely New Sweden Lutheran Church. The New Sweden community was settled around a cotton gin built by immigrants from Scandinavia, and fields filled with cotton and other crops still dominate the area. The Manda Schoolhouse, about a mile before the church, is a favorite starting point for cyclists exploring the more remote portions of this region.

There are historical markers along all three loops that recount the settlement of the area. The two longer rides pass settlements along Brushy Creek at Norman's Crossing and Rice's Crossing. The shorter ride turns south at the old Cele General Store, which along with the nearby Richland Hall and historic St. John's Lutheran Church are focal points for the residents of the surrounding Richland Community.

All three options use a hike-and-bike trail along Gilleland Creek to avoid city traffic for the final mile on the return to the park. Heavy rains cause flooding on the trail from time to time. If you choose to stay on the main roads back to town, be mindful of heavy traffic in this fast-growing area.

The Basics

Start: At Gilleland Creek Park in Pflugerville. Pflugerville is just north of Austin on I–35. To find the park, exit I–35 onto FM 1825 and continue straight (east) through town for 3.5 miles. Turn left onto Railroad Ave., also named the Pflugerville Loop, to the park.
Distance: Options of 50.0 miles, 37.1 miles, or 17.7 miles.
Terrain: Mostly flat, some gently rolling farmland.
Roads: Two-lane roads carrying mostly farm traffic. Some higher-speed traffic leaving Pflugerville on FM 685 and returning on Pflugerville East. Use the hike-and-bike trail for the last mile back into town to avoid traffic.

Food: Several options in Pflugerville; the Cele General Store may be open; two stores at Rice's Crossing; convenience store in Coupland.

Miles & Directions

- 0.0 Exit Gilleland Creek Park by turning left onto Railroad Ave., also known as Pflugerville Loop.
- 0.1 Turn immediately right onto Applewood Dr., a wide residential street, to avoid traffic.
- 0.3 Turn left onto Rocky Creek Dr. and follow it all the way to the end.
- 1.2 Turn right onto Pfennig La.
- 1.9 Turn left onto FM 685.
- 2.3 Turn right onto Pfluger La.
- 4.5 Cross cattle guard.
- 4.7 Cross another cattle guard at the intersection with Weiss La. Turn left onto Weiss La.
- 6.2 Weiss La. changes name to Cele Rd. as it curves right past Hodde La. Continue on Weiss/Cele.
- 8.5 Cameron Rd. merges with the Cele Rd. The Cele General Store is on this corner and may be available for provisions. Continue straight through stop sign and over small creek as road bends to the left.

For a shorter option totaling 17.7 miles, turn right onto Cameron Rd. at the Cele General Store. In 1.2 miles you'll pass Steger La. on the left. From here, follow the directions for the full tour from mile 41.9 to return to Pflugerville.

- 8.9 Cameron Rd. veers to the right at the intersection with Engerman La. Continue straight on Engerman La.
- 11.3 Continue straight on Engerman past the intersection of Melber La. Engerman La. becomes County Rd. 129 as you enter Williamson County.
- 12.7 Cross Brushy Creek.
- 13.1 At stop sign, turn right (east) onto FM 1660, at the Nor-

man's Crossing historical marker. Brushy Creek Baptist Church is on the left.

- 15.7 Stop sign at Rice's Crossing, with two stores at this corner. Turn right (south) on FM 973. Two lanes, some traffic, no shoulder.
- 17.7 Turn left onto Pfluger-Berkman Rd.
- 19.6 Pass Manda Rd. on the right.

For a shorter option totaling 37.1 miles, turn right onto Manda-Carlson Rd. After 1.7 miles you'll pass the intersection of Lund Rd. at a historical marker. From here, follow the directions for the full tour from mile 34.2 to return to Pflugerville.

- 20.4 Pfluger-Berkman Rd. changes name to County Rd. 458 as you cross the Williamson County line.
- 22.6 Cross Texas 95 onto Spur 277 and continue into Coupland.
- 23.3 Turn right onto FM 1466 and cross railroad tracks.

A convenience store is located 0.3 mile straight on Spur 277 past this intersection.

- 24.1 Turn right onto County Rd. 460.
- 26.8 Turn right onto County Rd. 461.
- 27.8 Turn right onto County Line Rd. (unmarked).
- 28.4 Carefully cross railroad tracks and Texas 95 to stay straight on County Line Rd.
- 29.3 Turn right onto Lund, careful of loose gravel at this turn.
- 34.2 Turn left onto Manda-Carlson Rd. past a historical marker. Note that this road's name changes to Manda Rd. at the other end.
- 36.3 Pass Manda School.
- 36.5 Turn right onto New Sweden Church Rd. Great view of the church. Pass New Sweden Lutheran Church (mile 37.6).
- 38.2 Continue on New Sweden Church Rd. as it bends left past the intersection with Axell Rd.
- 39.7 Pass New Sweden cemetery on the left. At the stop sign T intersection, turn right onto FM 973.

- 39.8 Turn left onto Steger La.
- 41.9 Turn left at the T intersection onto Cameron Rd.

The Cele General Store is 1.2 miles to the right.

- 42.2 Continue straight past the intersection with Jesse Bohls Rd.
- 42.4 Pass St. John's Church on the left.
- 44.2 Stay on Cameron as it bends right at the intersection with Fuchs Grove Rd. (unmarked) straight ahead.
- 46.4 Turn right onto Pflugerville East.
- 46.7 Pass intersection with Weiss La. on the right.
- 48.9 At the stoplight, turn left onto Dessau La. (Hutto Rd. is to the right.) Immediately (0.1 mile) after turning onto Dessau La. and crossing a bridge over Gilleland Creek, turn right into the Bohls Park parking lot. At the back of this small parking lot is a cement hike-and-bike trail, which will take you back to your starting point in 1 mile. Be mindful; Gilleland Creek, after heavy rains, may overflow the path.
- 49.9 Take the bike path to the left under the underpass of Pflugerville Loop Rd. where it branches in a Y.
- 50.0 Finish at Gilleland Creek Park.

14

Two Salado Rambles

Salado—Summers Mill—
Stillhouse Hollow Lake—Salado

Salado is a small village that traces its history back almost 150 years. The Chisholm Trail ran down Main Street in those days, and the town developed as a center for agriculture and trade.

A small, clear creek rises from an underground aquifer along the Balcones Fault and runs through the heart of Salado. Gristmills and cotton gins were built near Salado Creek, and hotels and stores prospered there until the turn of the century, when railroads that bypassed Salado were constructed.

Over the years Salado has been revitalized by the restoration of a variety of shops, historic sites, excellent restaurants, and charming bed-and-breakfasts. The restaurant at the Stagecoach Inn is among the oldest and best known, having hosted a long list of famous Texans and early travelers along the Chisholm Trail. Pleasant parks along the creek preserve the relaxed atmosphere of Salado.

The two Rambles set out here travel in opposite directions from Salado. One route heads east through fairly level farmland and ranch country, with several nice crossings of Salado Creek. You'll ride past some lovely horse farms, rural homes, and an especially scenic crossing of Salado Creek at Summers Mill.

A second route heads west through more challenging terrain toward the shores of Stillhouse Hollow Lake, which was created by a flood-control dam on the Lampasas River. This is a more difficult but equally rewarding route, passing through less-cultivated ranch land with distant Hill Country vistas. Combine these two options for a full day of cycling from Salado.

Bob Kelley recently moved his Spoke 'n Sprocket Bike Shop from Old Town Salado, where these Rambles start, to the nearby town of Killeen. Bob suggested these routes, and he can give you additional insight into cycling the area.

The Basics

Start: In Old Town Salado. Salado is 50 miles south of Waco and 50 miles north of Austin on I–35.
Length: Option one (east toward Summers Mill) is 23.0 miles. Option two (west toward Stillhouse Hollow Lake) is 30.7 miles.
Terrain: Gently rolling hills.
Roads: Lightly traveled FM and country roads.
Food: Several options in Salado.

Miles & Directions
Option One (east toward Summers Mill)

- 0.0 Exit Old Town Salado by turning right onto Main St.
- 0.6 Cross Salado Creek and pass two historical markers.
- 0.7 Turn left onto Royal St. and climb for 0.4 mile to the old water tower. Continue straight on Royal past some nice residences.
- 3.1 Continue straight on Royal through the intersection with Blackberry at the stop sign.
- 5.0 Turn right at the stop sign T intersection onto Armstrong. Possibility of loose gravel from farm equipment near this intersection.
- 6.3 Turn left at the stop sign T intersection onto FM 2268 (unmarked).
- 7.9 Turn left onto Krause, a great one-lane farm access road.
- 10.2 Continue on Krause as it bears right at the intersection with unpaved Barnes Rd.

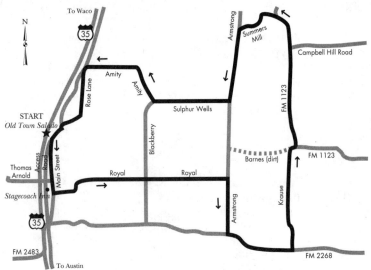

Option One (east toward Summers Mill)

Option Two (west toward Stillhouse Hollow Lake)

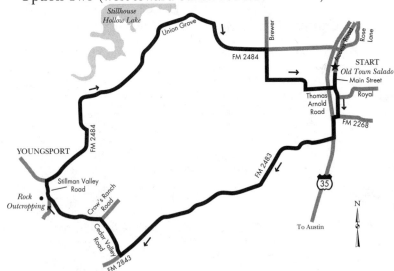

- 10.4 Turn hard left onto FM 1123 and pedal through open country for a few miles.
- 12.8 Continue straight through the intersection of Campbell Hill Rd., with airfield to the right and stables on the left.
- 13.4 As the road bends left, pass through a cluster of trees to the low-water crossing at Summers Mill.
- 13.7 Turn left onto Summers Mill past the entrance of Summers Mill Farm.
- 14.6 Turn left onto Armstrong at the T intersection; be mindful of loose gravel.
- 14.9 Cross Salado Creek.
- 16.3 Turn right onto Sulphur Wells. The Diamond S Farm is at this intersection.
- 18.0 A stop sign marks a T intersection with Blackberry to the left and Amity to the right. Turn right onto Amity.
- 18.2 Road narrows as it crosses Salado Creek. Begin a short climb after crossing the creek.
- 20.2 Amity reaches the access road to I–35. Make a left onto the access road, then another left onto Rose La. Rose La. bends right; its surface is a little rougher.
- 21.3 Continue on Rose La. by bearing right at the intersection with Stennett Mill.
- 22.0 Continue on Rose La. as it curves right past the intersection of Salado Park Rd.
- 22.1 Turn left onto the I–35 access road.
- 22.6 At the stop sign, turn left onto FM 2268, which is Main St. in Salado, and pass the road sign designating FM 2268 as the Texas Brazos Trail.
- 23.0 Finish in Old Town Salado.

Option Two (west toward Stillhouse Hollow Lake)

- 0.0 Exit Old Town Salado by turning right onto Main St.
- 1.3 After a short climb, Main St. merges with the access road to I–35 and FM 2843. Cross over I–35 on the overpass of FM 2843.

- 1.4 After crossing the overpass, turn left on FM 2843, which is also the southbound access road for I–35 for a short distance.
- 2.0 Turn right (west) on FM 2843 and go past a road sign warning of deer crossings for the next 11 miles. FM 2843 is a well-paved, two-lane road without a shoulder. Traffic is light but cars travel fast. Scenic vistas first begin around mile 5.5.
- 10.7 Turn right onto Cedar Valley Rd. (a church is at this corner), which is a narrower, more secluded road with a rougher surface, and pass through increasingly rolling countryside.
- 12.1 Stay left on Cedar Valley Rd. past the intersection with Crow's Ranch Rd.
- 14.1 Turn right onto Stillman Valley Rd. at the stop sign. This corner is marked by a prominent rock outcropping.
- 14.8 Descend to the intersection of Stillman Valley Rd. and FM 2484. Turn right and uphill onto FM 2484, which is another two-lane road with no shoulder but very little traffic.

0.3 mile to the left is a nice crossing of the Lampasas River to the community of Youngsport. Unfortunately, there are no stores in Youngsport.

- 22.4 Continue past turnoff for Union Grove Park. Some views of Stillhouse Hollow Lake appear in the distance.
- 23.5 Continue past intersection of Union Grove La. on the left and begin climbing for 1 mile.
- 26.4 Turn right onto Brewer, a more secluded country road.
- 27.5 Brewer bends sharply to the left and is renamed Thomas Arnold Rd. Continue on Thomas Arnold Rd.
- 30.0 Continue straight through the stop sign, across the I–35 access road, and over the overpass.
- 30.2 At the stop sign, turn left onto Main St.
- 30.7 Finish in Old Town Salado.

15

Hill Country
Flyer Challenge

Burnet—Bertram—Oatmeal—Marble Falls—
Mormon Mill—Burnet

The Hill Country Flyer is an excursion steam train that makes a sixty-mile round-trip from the town of Cedar Park (just north of Austin) to Burnet and back. It travels on a railway line built more than a hundred years ago to haul limestone, marble, and the pink granite used to build the Texas State Capitol from the stone quarries of Burnet County.

The train hauls tourists today, and it provides a unique way to reach Burnet and the starting point for both this route and the **Longhorn Caverns Cruise.** The train can transport bicycles by prior arrangement. Be sure to call ahead for reservations and to check scheduling.

This is the first of two bike rides beginning at the Burnet town square near the restored Hill Country Flyer train depot. There are fine country roads to ride in every direction from Burnet, another wonderful Hill Country town surrounded by beautiful countryside formed by an ancient and diverse geology. This route starts to the east, crossing the path of the Hill Country Flyer outside of Burnet.

After passing through ranch land on the way to Bertram and the rural Oatmeal community, the route turns south over increasingly hilly country. There are some dramatic and sweeping vistas in the distance as the road becomes steeper. A long, fabulous descent pre-

---

cedes a westward turn toward the town of Marble Falls. The final leg of this route travels north back to Burnet along the shaded and secluded Mormon Mill Road.

The exposed rock outcroppings visible along this ride through Burnet County, especially from RM 1174, are evidence of the forces of nature at work during the area's formation millions of years ago. A particularly grand view presents itself just before that long, fabulous descent near the halfway point of the full tour. From this vantage point, you'll get a good look at and feel for the rough and unspoiled beauty of Burnet County.

It's easy to imagine that the character of life along this rural route is little changed since the time of its first settlement, especially along the lovely Mormon Mill Road. In addition to stone quarrying, hunting and ranching have long been, and remain, the principal activities in this area. Be especially mindful of the popularity of hunting—and sensitive to private property rights—if you choose to explore this area during hunting season.

The Basics

Start: At the Burnet town square. Public parking is available around the county courthouse. Burnet is about 60 miles northwest of Austin.

Length: 56.2 miles. Riding to Bertram and returning through the Oatmeal community is 29.0 miles. There are two other opportunities to shorten the full tour slightly.

Terrain: Lots of rolling hills, mostly through open countryside. Portions of the Mormon Mill Rd. are shaded and secluded. Some climbing on RM 1174.

Roads: Quiet country roads. FM 1431 may have some traffic.

Food: Many options in Burnet, Bertram, and Marble Falls; Helen's Grocery is at mile 32.3 of the full tour.

Miles & Directions

- 0.0 Start at the corner of Pierce and Jackson and head east on Jackson St. toward the train depot.

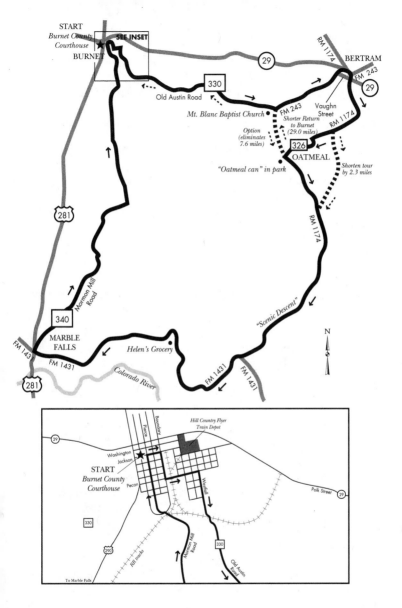

START
Burnet County
Courthouse
BURNET

SEE INSET

29

RM 1174

BERTRAM

FM 243

29

330

Old Austin Road

Mt. Blanc Baptist Church

FM 243

Vaughn
Street

*Shorter Return
to Burnet
(29.0 miles)*

RM 1174

*Option
(eliminates
7.6 miles)*

326

OATMEAL

"Oatmeal can" in park

*Shorten tour
by 2.3 miles*

RM 1174

281

"Scenic Descent"

N

340

Mormon Mill Road

MARBLE
FALLS

FM 143

FM 1431

Helen's Grocery

Colorado River

FM 1431

FM 1431

281

29

Pierce

Boundary

*Hill Country Flyer
Train Depot*

Washington
Jackson

START
*Burnet County
Courthouse*

Pecan

Westfall

Polk Street

29

330

290

BR tracks

Mormon Mill Road

330

Old Austin Road

To Marble Falls

- 0.2 Turn right (south) on Boundary St., just before the restored Hill Country Flyer depot.
- 0.4 Turn left (east) at stop sign onto Pecan St., immediately crossing railroad tracks.
- 0.7 Turn right (south) onto Westfall, also marked as Burnet County Rd. 330.
- 1.2 Pass underneath railroad overpass. Burnet County Rd. 330 at this point is also known as Old Austin Rd. Continue straight on Old Austin Rd. past the intersections with Burnet County Rd. 334 and Burnet County Rd. 332.
- 8.8 At the unmarked T intersection where the Old Austin Rd. ends, turn left onto FM 243. The Mount Blanc Baptist Church is on the right.

To shorten the full tour by 7.6 miles and bypass Bertram, turn right here. After 1.9 miles you'll pass the giant oatmeal can in the park on the right in Oatmeal. From that point, follow the directions from mile 18.3 of the full tour.

- 12.1 One block before FM 243 joins Texas 29, turn right onto Vaughn St. You'll parallel FM 243/Texas 29 through town and miss the traffic. There are stores along both Vaughn and FM 243/Texas 29.
- 12.5 At a stop sign, Vaughn St. rejoins FM 243/Texas 29 for only a few yards. Turn immediately right (south) onto RM 1174 at the Holy Cross Catholic Church.
- 15.4 Turn right onto Burnet County Rd. 326, a beautiful, narrow county road.

You can shorten the full tour by 2.3 miles by continuing straight on RM 1174. After 3.2 miles you'll pass the intersection of FM 243 to the right. Continue straight on RM 1174 and follow the directions for the full tour from mile 20.9.

- 17.4 Cross cattle guard.
- 18.1 Cross another cattle guard.
- 18.3 Turn left onto FM 243 (unmarked) at the giant oatmeal can in the park at Oatmeal.

For a shorter option totaling 29.0 miles, turn right onto FM 243. After 1.9 miles, turn left at the Mount Blanc Baptist Church onto Burnet County Rd. 330. Retrace your path back to Burnet in another 8.8 miles.

- 20.9 Bear right onto RM 1174.
- 21.7 Continue straight past intersection with RM 1869.
- 22.6 First of many beautiful vistas to come as you pass a road sign warning of steep grades (many, but not all, downhill) for the next 6 miles.
- 25.4 Begin a climb of 1 mile. At the top is a spectacular view and the start of a long, fabulous descent.
- 28.7 At T intersection, turn right onto FM 1431, a two-lane road with little or no shoulder and some traffic.
- 32.3 Pass Helen's Grocery on the left. There may be some continuing road construction coming out of Marble Falls as this road is widened.
- 41.2 Turn right at stoplight and ride briefly on US 281. There are options for food in all directions.
- 41.4 Turn right onto Mormon Mill Rd. This is a wonderful country road over rolling terrain, twisty and narrow in places, with very little traffic. Mormon Mill Rd. is marked in places as Burnet County Rd. 340. There will be three cattle guards to cross in the next 7 miles.
- 45.5 Continue straight past the intersection with Burnet County Rd. 341 to the right.
- 46.2 Road crosses Hamilton Creek and veers left, near the location of the original gristmill built by Mormon settlers in the 1850s.
- 53.7 Stay on Burnet County Rd. 340 as it veers right at intersection with Burnet County Rd. 340A.
- 55.5 Pass underneath a double railroad overpass and bear to the left after the second overpass.
- 55.6 Turn quickly right onto Pierce St.
- 56.2 End your tour at the Burnet town square.

16

Longhorn Caverns Cruise

*Burnet—Inks Lake State Park—Hoover Valley—
Longhorn Caverns State Park—Burnet*

This is the second of two routes starting at the Burnet town square near the restored Hill Country Flyer train depot. The focal points of this route through western Burnet County are the man-made lakes showcased in Inks Lake State Park and the natural caverns showcased in Longhorn Caverns State Park.

Riders looking for shorter routes have two options to choose from. One is to bypass the lakes by descending into the Hoover Valley and climbing toward Longhorn Caverns. The other is to bypass the caverns by climbing up out of the Hoover Valley after cycling past the lakes. Riders looking for longer routes can try a challenging out-and-back addition north into the hills that rise above the shore of Lake Buchanan.

These rides leave Burnet from the same place as the **Hill Country Flyer Challenge** but head in the opposite direction toward Lake Buchanan and Inks Lake. Lake Buchanan is the largest and northernmost of the man-made chain of Highland Lakes built to control flooding along the Colorado River from here all the way to Austin. After skirting the edge of Lake Buchanan, you'll enter the park road by Inks Lake, the second and smallest of these lakes.

There are several hills with scenic overlooks to climb and descend along the pretty park road before reaching the park entrance. There's an especially nice overlook into the park toward the Devil's Waterhole, a tempting spot to cool off if you're riding on a particularly hot day.

Past the park entrance is the Hoover Valley, denoted only by a historical marker and country store. As is often the case with valleys, the only way out is up. A shorter but more difficult option climbs the Hoover Valley Road back to Burnet. The climb toward Longhorn Caverns State Park is also substantial, as are the views of the countryside on the climb and from the top.

Viewed from the road, there is little to suggest something extraordinary at Longhorn Caverns State Park, but the underground caverns are one of a kind. The enormous chambers were carved slowly over time at the end of the Ice Age, and each has a colorful history of local use. A tour of the caverns, over a mile in length, takes about an hour and a half. There are also picnic areas and nature trails on the grounds of this unusual park, along with a coffee and gift shop.

The return to Burnet crosses open, quiet country and finishes along US 281, a road with higher-speed traffic but wide lanes. To avoid some of this traffic in town, the final two miles of the ride turn east to join the final two miles of the **Hill Country Flyer Challenge**, passing under the tracks of the steam train and back to the Burnet town square.

The Basics

Start: At the Burnet town square. There is parking around the Burnet County courthouse. Burnet is 60 miles northwest of Austin.

Length: 39.9 miles, with options of 33.9 miles and 27.2 miles. Additional miles are available by riding out-and-back on RM 2341.

Terrain: Gently rolling hills. Park Rd. 4 has steeper rolling hills and one very difficult climb before Longhorn Caverns State Park. Returning on the Hoover Valley Rd. (optional) involves steep climbs.

Roads: Texas 29 (used for 4.4 miles) and US 281 (used for 3.0 miles) are four-lane roads with high-speed traffic. Texas 29 has a poor shoulder but adequate room for traffic. The other roads are quiet country roads.

Food: Many choices in Burnet; convenience stores at the intersection of RM 690 and Texas 29 and on Park Rd. 4 just past the

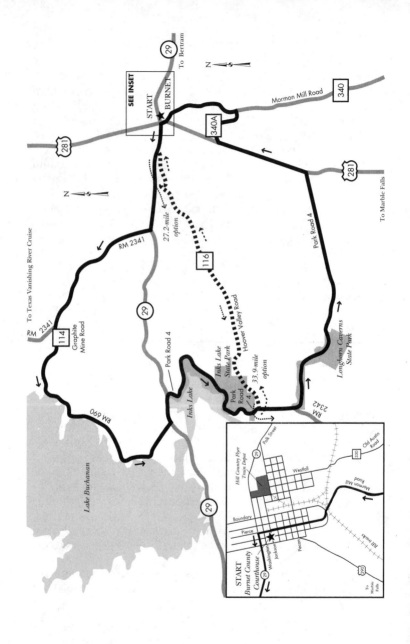

Hoover Valley Rd. The park headquarters at Inks Lake has water and restrooms. There is a coffee and gift shop at the Longhorn Caverns State Park administration building.

Miles & Directions

- 0.0 Leave Burnet town square from the corner of Washington St. and Pierce St., traveling north 1 block on Pierce.
- 0.1 At the stoplight, turn left off Pierce St. onto Texas 29 (also named Polk St. in town). Texas 29 is four lanes without shoulders.
- 0.2 Cross intersection of Texas 29 and US 281. Continue straight (west) through the stoplight on Texas 29.
- 2.2 To the left is Hoover Valley Rd., also marked as Burnet County Rd. 116.

For a shorter option totaling 27.2 miles, turn left onto Hoover Valley Rd., a narrow, secluded road through lovely ranch land. After about 6 miles, some dramatic views of Inks Lake and the surrounding countryside appear as you begin a steep descent. After 8.4 miles, Hoover Valley Rd. intersects with Park Rd. 4. Turn left onto Park Rd. 4 and follow the directions for the full tour from mile 23.3 to return to Burnet.

- 3.5 Turn right onto RM 2341, where a billboard directs you toward the Texas Vanishing River Cruise.
- 8.1 Turn left onto Graphite Mine Rd., which also is marked as Burnet County Rd. 114. You'll cross four cattle guards in the next 7 miles.

Note: Continuing straight on RM 2341 provides a challenging ride through quiet, hilly country, with lovely views of Lake Buchanan, toward the embarkation point of the Texas Vanishing River Cruise. Unfortunately the road dead-ends about 10 miles past Graphite Mine Rd. This is an excellent out-and-back course for cyclists looking to test their climbing abilities.

- 10.4 Bear left over a cattle guard as Burnet County Rd. 114 becomes RM 690.
- 16.2 Pass a convenience store and turn left onto Texas 29.
- 17.1 Turn right (south) onto Park Rd. 4 and enter Inks Lake State Park.
- 18.6 A scenic overlook is at the top of a short climb.
- 20.5 Pass the entrance to Inks Lake State Park on the right.
- 23.3 Pass the intersection of Hoover Valley Rd. (Burnet County Rd. 116) on the left.

For a shorter but more difficult option totaling 33.9 miles, turn left on the Hoover Valley Rd. and begin a long, steep climb out of the valley. The first 5 miles of this road are generally uphill, with an especially steep 1-mile climb beginning after 2.0 miles. After 8.4 miles turn right onto Texas 29, and after 10.6 miles finish at the Burnet town square. Note that a convenience store is on Park Rd. 4 only 0.3 mile past the Hoover Valley Rd. intersection.

- 23.6 Pass a convenience store on your left. A historical marker on the left near the Hoover Valley Cemetery (mile 24.1) dates Hoover Valley from 1850, when Reverend Issac Hoover founded a church here.
- 24.3 Bear left to stay on Park Rd. 4 where it intersects with RM 2342. Immediately begin a long, steep climb.
- 25.0 A picnic area with a great view is on the right at the top of the climb—a good place for a break.
- 26.9 Pass entrance to Longhorn Caverns State Park on the right.
- 32.9 Turn left onto US 281. This road has four lanes, a varying shoulder, and high-speed traffic. Continue on this road past the Burnet Airport, Museum, and Confederate Air Force Headquarters.
- 36.0 Turn right onto Burnet County Rd. 340A.

You can shorten this ride by 2 miles by continuing straight on US 281 to the intersection with Texas 29, turning right on Texas 29, and returning to the Burnet town square.

- 36.4 At stop sign, cross railroad tracks.
- 37.3 Turn left onto Burnet County Rd. 340.
- 39.2 Pass underneath double railroad overpass and bear immediately to the left.
- 39.3 Turn right onto Pierce St.
- 39.9 Finish at the Burnet town square.

North Texas
and the Piney Woods

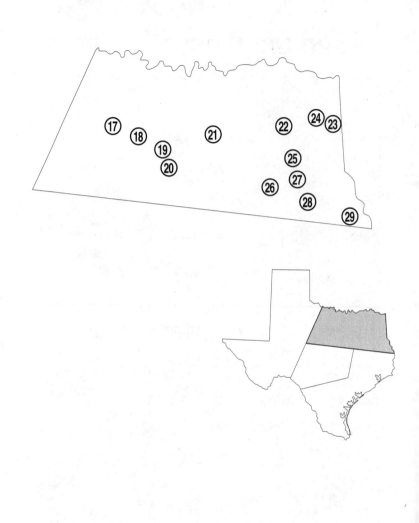

North Texas and the Piney Woods

17

Possum Kingdom Challenge

Possum Kingdom State Park—Caddo—Ivan—
Possum Kingdom State Park

Unusually clear water is one of the unique features of Lake Possum Kingdom, a popular destination for scuba divers and campers from across the Southwest. The lake was formed by damming the Brazos River, but the river had long before carved deep canyons through the limestone and sandstone beds here. This beautiful lake and its canyon walls and cliffs are on display throughout Possum Kingdom State Park, the starting point for this ride through the countryside to the west and south of the lake.

Another unique feature in the park is a large portion of the official state longhorn herd. Longhorn cattle once ran wild across Texas but were nearly bred out of existence on domestic ranches. A pure strain of this distinctive symbol of Texas is preserved in some Texas state parks, including the park at Possum Kingdom. Much of the countryside you'll ride through on this route is high-quality range land where ranching continues to be the principal activity.

Possum Kingdom State Park is on the lake's west side, about twenty miles south of the town of Graham. Longer routes through this area can be fashioned starting in or passing through Graham. There are also good roads to cycle on the east side of the lake. Although Possum Kingdom State Park may seem like a remote starting point, it allows for a special ride on a long, quiet park road.

The ride begins with a climb out of the park through a pretty, wooded canyon and continues south along the park road for sixteen miles to the community of Caddo. Happily there is a general store in Caddo and a chance to stock up before turning west and north through open range country. At the northwest corner of this loop is the community of Ivan, notable to hungry cyclists as the location of Daddy D's Barbeque.

The route turns east from Ivan then south onto FM 3253 before rejoining the park road back to Possum Kingdom. Before turning south you can add even more miles with an out-and-back by continuing east on FM 1148 along the north shore of the lake. The pavement eventually ends, but there is a convenience store and some good lookout points toward the lake along the way.

The Basics

Start: At the entrance to Possum Kingdom State Park, on the west side of Lake Possum Kingdom. The park is about 20 miles south of Graham. Graham is about 90 miles northeast of Abilene and 90 miles northwest of Fort Worth.

Distance: 48.9 miles, with more miles available out-and-back toward the north shore of the lake.

Terrain: Big climb out of the park; rolling hills along the park road; flat, open stretches with some hills along the FM roads.

Roads: Park and FM roads are two lanes, no shoulder, but very light traffic. Short stretch on US 180 has a wide shoulder.

Food: Caddo Mercantile store in Caddo; Daddy D's Barbeque in Ivan; seasonal concessions at the park.

Miles & Directions

- 0.0 Exit Possum Kingdom State Park on Park Rd. 33. You'll cross two cattle guards in the first 2 miles.
- 8.1 Stay on Park Rd. 33 south past the junction of FM 3253 to the right.
- 16.0 Pass Caddo town sign.
- 16.3 At the stop sign intersection, turn left onto Texas Loop 252, following the sign to the Caddo Mercantile store.
- 17.1 Caddo Mercantile is at stop sign intersection with US 180.

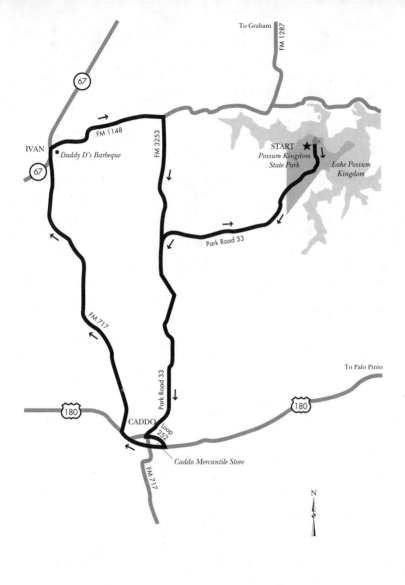

Turn right (west) onto US 180, which has four lanes and a wide shoulder.

- 17.7 Continue straight as FM 717 (north) merges with US 180 west.
- 18.9 Turn right to follow FM 717 north, which has two lanes and no shoulder.
- 30.1 At stop sign intersection, turn right (north), where FM 717 merges with Texas 67. Two lanes and some shoulder.
- 30.7 Pass Ivan town sign and Daddy D's Barbeque, then turn right (east) onto FM 1148.
- 35.6 Turn right (south) onto FM 3253, which has two lanes and no shoulder.

For a longer ride, continue straight (east) here on FM 1148 toward the lake. In 5 miles there is a convenience store, just before the road begins to parallel the north shore of Lake Possum Kingdom. There are some great overlooks as the road continues for several miles before the pavement ends.

- 40.7 FM 3253 ends, merging with Park Rd. 33. At stop sign, turn left (north) on Park Rd. 33. Two lanes, no shoulder, rolling hills.
- 46.7 Cross first of two cattle guards; begin long descent toward park.
- 48.9 Finish at the park entrance.

18

Palo Pinto Ramble

Palo Pinto—Lake Palo Pinto—
Lone Camp—Palo Pinto

The tiny town of Palo Pinto takes its name from the beautiful natural features found throughout Palo Pinto County. Palo Pinto Creek is dammed to form Lake Palo Pinto to the south. Limestone outcroppings prominent to the east are known to geologists as the Palo Pinto formation, and Palo Pinto is the name of a colorful building stone found here. The town sits on the edge of a small range known locally as the Palo Pinto Mountains. On this ride you'll start in the town, cross the creek, ride along the lake shore, pass the outcroppings, and climb in the small range.

A favorite feature of this ride is the wooded canyon you'll climb through at the end of the route. This route is described in a counterclockwise direction from town to save the prettiest part of the ride (and the one store along the way) for last. To enjoy the best portion of this ride right away, consider riding the route in a clockwise direction, starting with a nice descent.

Palo Pinto is as small as any county seat visited on the tours in this book. There is a county courthouse, which marks the start of the ride, a convenience store and a police station across the street, and a barbeque restaurant open for lunch during the week. Mineral Wells is the largest nearby town, eleven miles to the east on US 180.

For a larger starting place and a longer ride, you might consider riding US 180 out-and-back from Mineral Wells. Although the road traffic is fast, the shoulder on US 180 is extremely wide, the terrain is quite challenging, and many of the views are lovely. There is parking on the west side of Mineral Wells, closest to Palo Pinto, at a city park 10.8 miles from the Palo Pinto County courthouse or in the lot across from Mineral Wells High School, 11.5 miles from the Palo Pinto County courthouse.

The counterclockwise route from the Palo Pinto County courthouse continues on US 180 for a few miles before turning onto two-lane roads. The first portion of the ride in this direction is fairly unassuming, but at the nine-mile mark, you come to a nice descent and the special character of this route begins. There is hilly terrain covered with foliage displaying some nice colors in the fall. There are good views of the lake, which is filled with migratory ducks and birds in winter. At the end, there's that spectacular climb through the shaded canyon back to Palo Pinto.

The Basics

Start: In front of the Palo Pinto County courthouse. Palo Pinto is 10 miles west of Mineral Wells on US 180.
Distance: 28.5 miles.
Terrain: Rolling hills, with a long climb near the finish.
Roads: US 180 has a wide shoulder; FM roads are two lanes, no shoulder, light traffic.
Food: Don's Grocery in Palo Pinto; store in Lone Camp.

Miles & Directions

- 0.0 Begin in front of courthouse on US 180, heading left (west) on US 180, which is also south on FM 4 here. US 180 is marked as the Texas Forts Trail.
- 0.3 Continue straight on US 180 past turnoff for FM 4 south on the left.
- 5.1 Turn left (south) carefully across traffic onto FM 919, through open range country.

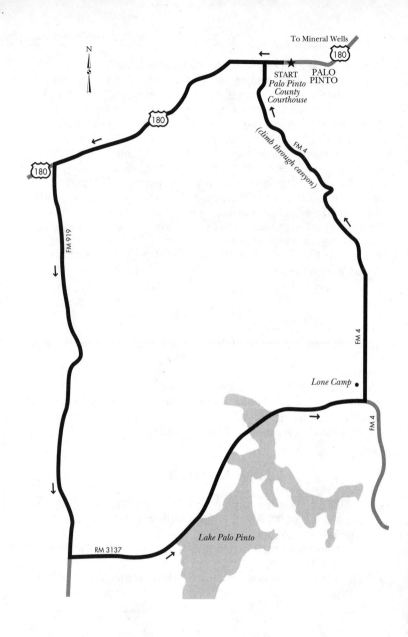

- 9.1 Descent marks change in character of terrain.
- 13.1 Turn left (east) onto RM 3137.
- 15.5 Pass shore of Lake Palo Pinto.
- 16.1 After cresting a hill, the large structure you see in the distance is a power plant.
- 17.3 First causeway along lakeshore by the power plant.
- 18.0 Second causeway along lakeshore with power plant behind.
- 18.7 Palo Pinto Marina may be open seasonally for something to drink.
- 20.6 Turn left (north) onto FM 4 at stop sign T intersection.
- 21.0 Enter community of Lone Camp and pass convenience store.
- 23.2 Prettiest part of route begins with a descent as the surrounding woods and hills close in on the road.
- 24.5 Begin a climb of about 1.5 miles.
- 27.8 Pass Palo Pinto town sign.
- 28.2 Turn left (east) at stop sign intersection with US 180.
- 28.5 Finish at Palo Pinto County courthouse.

19

Granbury Cruise

Granbury—Thorpe Spring—Tin Top—
Spring Creek—Baker—Granbury

Like Jefferson in east Texas and Fredericksburg in the Texas Hill Country, Granbury is an attractive and interesting small town in a beautiful setting, providing a great base for cycling in all directions. Granbury is located on the edge of the Glen Rose Formation, and the **Dinosaur Valley Ramble** starts about fifteen miles to the south. This route explores the countryside to the north, past Lake Granbury and through some quiet, secluded ranch land.

Granbury was established in the mid-nineteenth century as a trading post on the Brazos River. In 1969 the Brazos River was dammed to form Lake Granbury, and resorts sprung up quickly along more than 100 miles of shoreline. A restoration began in the small town as well, and today Granbury is a popular tourist and resort community.

Restored historic buildings housing cozy inns and bed-and-breakfasts are tucked away throughout Granbury. The bed-and-breakfast association or visitors bureau (800–950–2212) can direct you to some unique places to stay if you decide on a longer visit. The Granbury Opera House has been active since the mid-1970s, and there is lots of shopping, interesting museums, and nice places to eat after your ride.

This route begins at the town square around the Hood County courthouse. There is public parking around the courthouse, but if you visit on weekends or during holidays, you'll find parking difficult. Look for additional parking behind the town square to the north, near the train depot and city park.

Leaving Granbury you'll ride on FM roads past Thorpe Spring and over hilly terrain with some glimpses of Lake Granbury to the east. After an especially nice crossing of the Brazos River, you'll turn onto quieter country roads through the community of Tin Top. Past Tin Top, the course turns back toward Granbury through the Spring Creek and Baker communities.

There is surprising variety along the eight miles you'll travel on the isolated Baker Road. The countryside here alternately displays narrow, wooded corridors, open fields, rolling hills, and water crossings. At the end of Baker Road, you'll pass some nice looking ranches, many marked by signs proudly proclaiming their establishment in the 1850s.

The ride returns to Granbury with nine miles on FM 51, marked as part of the Texas Lakes Trail. Although the speed of traffic increases, the road has an adequate shoulder for bikes for its entire length. There are some nice lake views and crossings on this final stretch.

Stephanie James manages the Bike Rack, Granbury's bicycle shop. Pay her a visit to learn about other good roads to ride on your visit to the Granbury area.

The Basics

Start: In front of the Hood County courthouse. Mileage is marked from the corner of FM 4/FM 51 north where it diverges with US 377/FM 51 south. Granbury is 30 miles southwest of Fort Worth on US 377.

Distance: 41.7 miles or 36.4 miles.

Terrain: Rolling hills.

Roads: FM 2580 is two lanes, no shoulder, with some traffic. Traffic is heavier on FM 51, but there is a wide shoulder that narrows over the lake crossing. Little traffic on Tin Top Rd. and Baker La. Tin Top Rd. has some rough surfaces.

Food: Many options in Granbury and leaving town in Thorpe

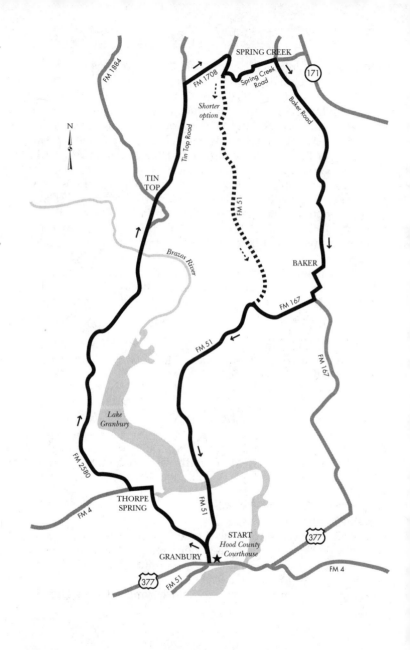

Spring. Two restaurants and a convenience store in Tin Top. Limited hours for Alicia's Burrito Hut on FM 51.

Miles & Directions

- 0.0 Exit town square north on FM 4/FM 51, also called Houston St.
- 0.4 Cross railroad tracks and turn left (north) onto FM 4, also called Lipan Rd.
- 3.8 Pass the Pocket Change convenience store and turn right (north) onto FM 2580, also called the Tin Top Hwy. Hilly road with two lanes, no shoulder, and with long views into surrounding countryside past water "tanks" and glimpses of Lake Granbury to the right.

You may encounter several dogs on this part of the ride.

- 12.5 Nice views as you descend toward and cross the Brazos River.
- 13.6 Pass Tin Top town sign.
- 14.2 At four-way intersection, go straight onto Tin Top Rd., past Mary's Brazos Café on left. This intersection features a convenience store, Cody's Country Café, Old Tin Top Rd. to the right, and FM 1884 (unmarked) to the left. Country lane, no shoulder.
- 17.9 Turn right (east) onto FM 1708. This intersection is poorly marked, but you'll see a large sign for the Precious Pasture Goat Farm on the right.
- 19.5 Turn right (east) onto FM 51 at stop sign T intersection. Wide shoulder, two lanes.
- 20.1 Turn left carefully across traffic at sign for Spring Creek onto Spring Creek Rd. Great country lanes; very isolated.

For a shorter option totaling 36.4 miles, continue straight on FM 51 all the way back to the Granbury town square. The ride along Baker Rd. is well worth the extra 5 miles, though.

- 22.1 At stop sign intersection, turn right onto Baker Rd.
- 22.8 Stay on Baker Rd. by bearing left at Y intersection with Floyd Rd.
- 28.2 At the Baker Baptist Church, bear left and stay on Baker Rd. at the Y intersection with the Baker Cut-Off.
- 30.4 Turn right onto FM 167, also called the Temple Hall Hwy., at stop sign T intersection. As you've just crossed a county line, the road signs here say you're exiting Gray Rd./Hood County Rd. 410.
- 32.7 At stop sign T intersection, turn left (south) onto FM 51, also called the Weatherford Hwy. You might be able to get some food or a drink at Alicia's Burrito Hut if you're riding early in the day.
- 37.7 Pass convenience store.
- 39.3 Shoulder narrows as you cross Lake Granbury (0.3-mile crossing).
- 41.3 Cross railroad tracks.
- 41.7 Finish at Granbury town square.

20

Dinosaur Valley Ramble

Glen Rose—Dinosaur Valley State Park—
Paluxy—Glen Rose

Many of the routes in this book are designed to follow the paths of earlier travelers through Texas, whether they were explorers seeking conquest, settlers starting new lives, or traders in search of new markets. This ride along the Paluxy River and through the Glen Rose Formation follows the tracks of even earlier inhabitants, those left behind by dinosaurs more than a hundred million years ago.

Glen Rose is a small town located in a lovely area about an hour's drive southwest of Fort Worth. Established in the mid-nineteenth century as a trading post, Glen Rose is now the county seat of one of Texas's lesser populated counties. There are restored bed-and-breakfasts to stay in, pretty parks to visit, and terrific roads to ride.

The geology of the surrounding countryside—known as the Glen Rose Formation—consists of alternating layers of sandstone, limestone, and shale deposited by the shallow seas that once covered Texas. Footprints of the dinosaurs that roamed the area remain imbedded in this soft stone and can be seen throughout Dinosaur Valley State Park, which you'll pass five miles into your ride. The park is an excellent place to learn about these prints and the dinosaurs that made them.

After leaving Glen Rose and passing the state park, you'll roll through wooded countryside. The higher elevations along this route have a Hill Country look and feel, with grasses and shrubs prominent among small limestone outcroppings. The lower elevations near the river bottomlands support larger trees and more lush vegetation. The area also is known as a habitat for an unusually wide variety of birds, some of which are listed as endangered species.

Halfway into the route you'll turn onto Somervell County roads, which are well maintained and very quiet. All the county roads in Somervell County are paved, and there is more good cycling nearby, especially to the south and west. The country lanes described here access nicely kept ranches and offer some terrific views near the river and into the surrounding hills from high points. Although the return into Glen Rose is along a road with higher-speed traffic, it offers a wide shoulder and more nice views.

Should you decide to try the shorter route, heed a special caution suggested by one of the state park rangers who sometimes bicycles to work. There are two low-water crossings of the Paluxy River on Somervell County Road 1008 shortly after leaving FM 205. These crossings have exquisite views but are tricky to navigate and can be very dangerous if the river is running high. Walk these crossings under all circumstances and exercise care and good judgment, depending on conditions and your ability, in deciding whether to cross at all. The full tour passes a few yards from the second crossing on the other side of the river.

The Basics

Start: Glen Rose, in front of the Somervell County courthouse. Glen Rose is about 75 miles southwest of Dallas on US Highway 67.
Distance: 27.1 miles or 15.1 miles.
Terrain: Gently rolling terrain along county roads. Some hills on FM roads.
Roads: County roads are narrow, well maintained, lightly traveled. FM 205 and FM 51 are two lanes, no shoulder, light traffic. FM 56 has a wide shoulder.
Food: Several options in Glen Rose; water at ranger station in park; store 0.2 mile off the route at the intersection of FM 56 near Post Oak Chapel.

Miles & Directions

- 0.0 Head west from the Somervell County courthouse where FM 56—also called Barnard St.—and FM 205 converge.
- 0.1 Continue straight (west) on FM 205 as FM 56 veers to the right.
- 1.6 At stop sign intersection, carefully cross US 67. Across US 67, FM 205 is also called Park Rd. 59.
- 3.7 Cross Paluxy River and pass first of several privately owned displays of dinosaur tracks, called "Creations Evidence Museum."
- 4.4 Pass entrance to Dinosaur Valley State Park to the right. It's 0.7 mile down the park road to the ranger station.
- 5.0 Nice view and descent after a climb, past more private displays of dinosaur tracks.
- 5.6 Pass junction with Somervell County Rd. 1008 on the right.

For a shorter option totaling 15.1 miles, turn right onto Somervell County Rd. 1008. There are water crossings after 0.2 mile and 0.9 mile and a lovely ride along the river and past the Lanham Mills cemetery in between. After 1 mile, turn right onto Somervell County Rd. 1007 and follow directions for the full tour from mile 18.6 to return to Glen Rose. CAUTION: Always walk the two water crossings on this route. They can be slippery.

- 10.5 Turn right (north) at stop sign T intersection as FM 205 merges with FM 51.
- 12.4 Stay on FM 51 as FM 205 veers left and the terrain becomes hillier.
- 12.9 Pass town sign for the community of Paluxy.
- 13.5 After crossing a sizable bridge, turn right onto Edwards Rd. When you cross the county line from Hood to Somervell in 1.5 miles, this road is named Somervell County Rd. 1008.
- 16.9 *CAUTION:* A small low-water crossing comes up quickly here as the approach is downhill and around a curve. Walk this crossing.

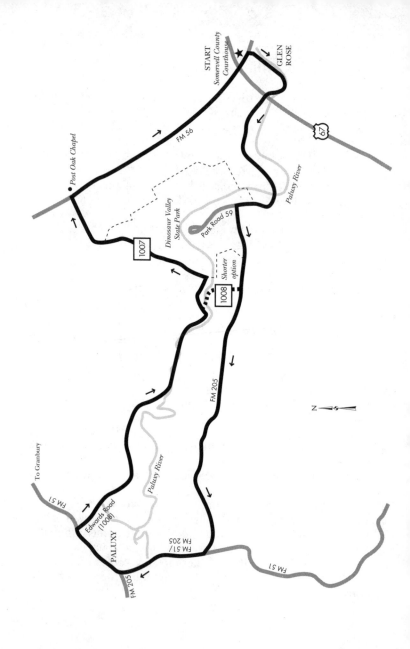

START
Somervell County
Courthouse

GLEN
ROSE

67

FM 56

Post Oak Chapel

Paluxy River

Dinosaur Valley
State Park

1007

Park Road 59

Shorter
option

1008

FM 205

N

FM 205

To Granbury

FM 51

Edwards Road
(1008)

Paluxy River

PALUXY

FM 51/
FM 205

FM 205

FM 51

FM 51

- 17.7 Pavement may be washed out along a section of 0.2 mile that is closed in by the river on one side and bluffs on the other.
- 18.6 Turn left at Y intersection onto Somervell County Rd. 1007. The shorter option rejoins the full tour here.
- 22.4 Turn right at stop sign T intersection onto FM 56, which is unmarked here. Post Oak Memory Chapel is at this intersection.

A convenience store is 0.2 mile to the left.

- 26.6 Continue straight through stoplight intersection with US 67. FM 56 is also called Hereford St. here.
- 27.0 Turn left at stop sign as FM 56 merges with FM 205/ Barnard St.
- 27.1 Finish at Somervell County courthouse.

21

White Rock Ramble

Valley View Park—White Rock Lake—
Valley View Park

The Dallas Park and Recreation Department maintains several bike trails in the Dallas metropolitan area. The two longest and most popular trails—one along White Rock Creek and the other around White Rock Lake—join in north central Dallas. As a result of community commitment to and civic pride in these trails, excellent bike rides are possible in the heart of one of Texas's largest cities.

The White Rock Trails are a tribute to aggressive planning, active management, and attention to detail. Trail supervisor David Young and other members of the Park and Recreation Department have accumulated a unique insight and special expertise into the needs and safety of urban trail users. These paths are the result of years of operation and problem solving and are acclaimed as models for successful urban trails.

A surprising number of variables must be addressed to maintain a safe and usable urban trail way. Design features include water fountains set twenty-five feet back from the trail way and unobstructed shoulders for passing and leeway. Other features, such as the design and placement of curves and corners and the absence of tunnels, are more subtle but equally important considerations.

The trail along White Rock Creek has a concrete surface with many small wooden bridges spanning creek crossings. The trail usually continues uninterrupted by passing under busy streets, but the few traffic intersections are well regulated with traffic signals or signs. There are stone mileage markers along the way and the path is clearly marked. The trail parallels White Rock Creek along much of its length, passing through some forested areas and smaller parks as you approach the lake.

The trail around White Rock Lake is a combination of concrete and paved surfaces, portions of which are rough. The trail merges with roadways at times but is well marked and logical to follow. White Rock Lake, which was impounded in the early 1900s, is almost always in view from the trail.

The Park and Recreation Department lists the trail distance around White Rock Lake at 9.33 miles. Since there are several opportunities to ride on a wider roadway parallel to the trail, an exact distance for your ride may be hard to measure. However, differences are small, usually no more than a few tenths of a mile.

These trails are "multi-user" trails; that is, they are designed to accommodate joggers, roller bladers, and an occasional horseback rider. They are narrower than a roadway, and some sections see heavy use from time to time. Because of these multiple uses, the trail's popularity, and its urban setting, you should be especially attentive to courtesy and safety in sharing the trail with others.

For a copy of trail-use guidelines or more information about Dallas bike trails, call the Dallas Park and Recreation Department at (214) 670–8351 or write them at 7803 Fair Oaks, Dallas 75231.

The Basics

Start: At the Valley View Park, corner of Hillcrest Rd. and Valley View La. in north central Dallas. The park can be reached from the LBJ Frwy. White Rock Lake is 3 miles east of the Central Expwy. on Mockingbird La.

Distance: 23.2 miles; 16.2 miles starting from Harry S. Moss Park; laps around White Rock Lake are 9.0 miles.

Terrain: Flat.

Roads: A concrete trail from Valley View Park to White Rock Lake; trail around the lake is paved; there are many wooden bridge crossings along the way.

Food: Water fountains along the trail.

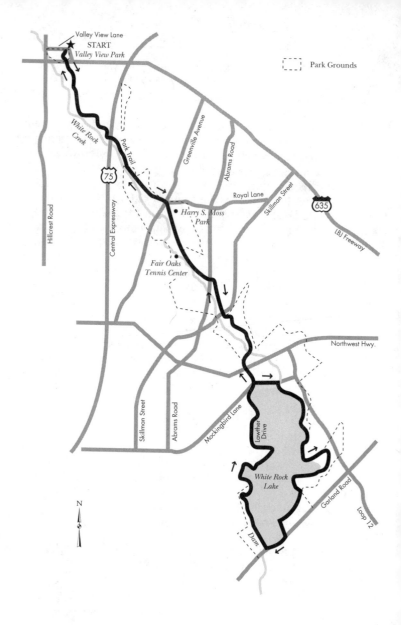

Valley View Lane
START
Valley View Park

Park Grounds

White Rock Creek

Park Trail

75

Central Expressway

Greenville Avenue

Abrams Road

Royal Lane

Skillman Street

635

LBJ Freeway

• Harry S. Moss Park

• Fair Oaks Tennis Center

Northwest Hwy.

Hillcrest Road

Skillman Street

Abrams Road

Mockingbird Lane

Lawther Drive

White Rock Lake

Garland Road

Loop 12

Dam

N

Miles & Directions

- 0.0 Start at Valley View Park entrance to the park trail.
- 0.4 Pass LBJ Frwy.
- 2.1 Pass under Central Expwy.
- 2.7 Pass under Royal La.
- 3.3 Enter Northwood Park.
- 3.5 Pass Harry S. Moss Park at the corner of Greenville Ave. and Royal La. Parking here makes this a good alternate starting point for a shorter ride.
- 5.0 Pass Fair Oaks Tennis Center.
- 5.2 Continue straight at intersection with a trail spur to the left.
- 5.3 Pass under Abrams Rd.
- 5.8 Pass under Skillman St.
- 6.3 Double creek crossing.
- 6.4 Pass under railroad tracks.
- 6.6 Cross Lawther Dr.
- 6.8 At traffic light cross Northwest Hwy.
- 7.1 Turn left at the corner of West Lawther Dr. and Mockingbird La. to circle clockwise around White Rock Lake.
- 8.1 Bike path is unmarked for a few tenths of a mile as it merges with E. Lawther Dr.
- 9.5 Pass corner of Tiffany Way and E. Lawther Dr.
- 9.9 Pass corner of Poppy Dr. and E. Lawther Dr.
- 10.3 Trail pulls away from lakeshore briefly around a hill with a building at the top. Staying on the roadway adds 0.2 mile along the lakeshore. At this point the bike lane is to the left of oncoming traffic, so for the next 1.5 miles, you might be passed by oncoming car traffic to your right and oncoming bike traffic to your left.
- 10.6 Turn left on the trail at the corner of Lawther Dr. and Winfrey Pt.
- 11.5 Turn right at corner of Garland Rd. and E. Lawther. Nice lake crossing and downhill past spillway.
- 12.1 Trail turns right at the corner of Winstead Dr. and Garland Rd.

- 12.2 After crossing a wooden bridge, a short climb to the lake dam is the only real elevation on the route.
- 12.8 Leaving the dam, pass redbrick waterworks built in 1911.
- 13.2 Past wooden bridge and abandoned boathouse.
- 13.6 This stretch of the trail parallels Lawther, where many cyclists take to the main road.
- 16.1 Complete circuit of White Rock Lake at the corner of West Lawther Dr. and Mockingbird La., turn left on trail, and retrace your steps to return to Valley View Park.

Additional loops around White Rock Lake add 9.0 miles each to your ride.

- 16.4 At traffic light cross Northwest Hwy.
- 16.6 Cross Lawther Dr.
- 16.8 Pass under railroad tracks.
- 16.9 Double creek crossing.
- 17.4 Pass under Skillman St.
- 17.9 Pass under Abrams Rd.
- 18.0 Bear left at Y intersection with a trail spur.
- 18.2 Pass Fair Oaks Tennis Center.
- 19.7 Pass Harry S. Moss Park at the corner of Greenville Ave. and Royal La.
- 19.9 Enter Northwood Park, golf course to the left.
- 20.5 Pass under Royal La.
- 21.1 Pass under Central Expwy.
- 23.2 Finish at Valley View Park, corner of Hillcrest Rd. and Valley View La.

22

Autumn Trails Ramble

Winnsboro—Chalybeatye Springs—
Perryville—Winnsboro

Wood County is laced with lovely country lanes weaving through thick forests. The town of Winnsboro, which straddles the county line to the north, makes a good starting point for a bike ride through the woods to the south.

Ever since its founding at the crossroads of two early trade routes, Winnsboro has been billed as "trails country." In the late 1950s, the town began a celebration of this heritage each October with tours through the woods past local points of interest. Over the years, Winnsboro's Autumn Trails have become one of the best-known tributes to fall foliage in Texas.

Today there are several routes for the Autumn Trails tours. The bike route described here closely follows the original tour, which is to the southeast of town. It's an attractive route at any time of the year. In the spring, blooming dogwood trees and wildflowers add special color. In the summer, most of the route is thickly shaded. In the fall, of course, the changing colors in the forest are a main attraction.

The course begins on a main road toward a historical marker for Chalybeatye Springs, whose waters briefly supported a small resort community. Here you'll turn into the woods on the first of these narrow Wood County roads. A shorter option stays on the county roads and loops back to Winnsboro. The full tour continues south on an FM road to the community of Perryville; then it returns to town on a long stretch through the forest.

Parts of the Wood County roads have rough surfaces, but there's usually so little traffic that you can pick your way with relative ease. The county roads are narrow in spots and visibility is limited because the trees crowd in so close to the roadside. On the hillier and more twisted sections, keep the possibility of oncoming traffic in mind.

This area is filled with nearby lakes, both large and small, that are favored by bass fishermen. If you decide to spend some time in this area and want to see some of this lake country by bike, there are more good roads to explore on the north side of Winnsboro in Franklin County, near Mount Vernon and Lake Cypress Springs.

The Basics

Start: Near the Chamber of Commerce building in Winnsboro. Look for parking there, behind the bank next door, at the Heritage Mall, or at other spots nearby. Distances are measured from the convergence of Texas 37/Texas 11/FM 852.

Distance: 28.9 miles or 16.0 miles.

Terrain: Flat to gently rolling, with some climbing on Wood County Rd. 4560.

Roads: Wood County roads are narrow lanes with some rough surfaces and little traffic. Trees come right up to the side of the road. Other roads are two lanes, no shoulder, light traffic.

Food: Several options in Winnsboro.

Miles & Directions

- 0.0 Leave intersection of Texas 37/Texas 11/FM 852 by heading east on Texas 11.
- 0.7 Pass Autumn Trails Park and Rodeo to the right.
- 1.6 Cross railroad tracks.
- 3.7 At corner with historical marker for Chalybeatye Springs to the left and a barbeque place to the right, turn right onto County Rd. 4430, a narrow lane with some rough surface.

- 6.0 Turn left (east) at stop sign intersection with FM 852 (unmarked here). Two lanes, no shoulder; lots of cows, horses, and trees in the fields.

For a shorter option totaling 16.0 miles, continue straight across this intersection onto County Rd. 4560. After 0.8 mile, you'll reach the Y intersection with County Rd. 4530. Turn right onto County Rd. 4530 and resume directions for the full tour at mile 19.7 to return to Winnsboro.

- 12.0 Continue past junction of FM 1647 to the left. Road is marked as part of the Texas Forest Trail.
- 12.5 Pass Perryville town sign.
- 12.8 Pass convenience store.
- 12.9 At stop sign T intersection, turn right (west) onto FM 2088, marked as Texas Forest Trail.
- 14.2 Turn right onto County Rd. 4560, a narrow lane with some rough surface through a hilly, thick forest.
- 14.6 Bear left to stay on County Rd. 4560, then pass intersection of County Rd. 4579 to left and go downhill through very thick forest.
- 15.9 Especially rough spot in the road.
- 16.4 Cross cattle guard.
- 17.1 Cross cattle guard and bear left to stay on County Rd. 4560 at the intersection with County Rd. 4570.
- 19.7 Turn back with a hard left at Y intersection onto County Rd. 4530, crossing some rough pavement. The shorter option rejoins here.
- 22.6 Turn right onto FM 2869 (unmarked here). Two lanes, no shoulder. The thick woods give way to nice pastures.
- 26.6 At stop sign T intersection, turn left (west) onto FM 852.
- 27.1 Pass Winnsboro town sign.
- 27.5 At stop sign junction with FM 515, turn left (west); some traffic entering town.
- 28.2 Continue straight through stoplight where FM 852/FM 515/FM 312 all meet.
- 28.4 Turn right at stoplight for Texas 37.
- 28.9 Cross railroad tracks and finish.

23

Caddo Lake Cruise

Jefferson—Caddo Lake State Park—Jefferson

You may be surprised to find a major nineteenth-century seaport beautifully preserved in the forests near the borders of Louisiana and Arkansas. Historic Jefferson has a unique look and feel and is among the most charming small towns in the state. It is a fun place to visit and makes a great base for cycling and sightseeing in northeast Texas.

Jefferson sits on Big Cypress Bayou near the western shore of Caddo Lake, a huge naturally formed lake that spreads eastward into Louisiana. In the early nineteenth century, logs and debris clogged the waterways here, keeping water levels high enough for steamboats to navigate through the bayous, lakes, and rivers from Jefferson all the way to New Orleans.

Rich plantation lands surrounded Jefferson, whose early character and heritage was more southern than southwestern. Jefferson served as the area's business center, and it quickly became one of the busiest and most prosperous towns in the early years of Texas statehood.

Eventually, river channels were cleared, water levels dropped, and railroads became the principal means of moving commerce. Jefferson is no longer a major commercial center, but its restored downtown maintains some of the atmosphere and feel of a prosperous nineteenth-century river port. The town center has some wonderful inns, shops, restaurants, and historic sites, and there are restored buildings of interest throughout the town.

This bike route heads east from Jefferson, through pastures cleared from the woods, to the Caddo Lake State Park. The unusual park is thickly forested and laced with swampy, cypress-filled bayous not far from the main body of the lake. A ride along the peaceful park road contains some marvelous views into a forest of moss-covered trees abundant with birds and wildlife.

The park is a Civilian Conservation Corps project built during the Depression. In those days, the park was one of the few ways the public had access to the lake, the majority of the surrounding land being privately owned. Much of the park land was donated by T. J. Taylor, a major landowner in the neighboring town of Karnack and the father of Lady Bird Johnson.

Life along the lake is particularly peaceful, and the nearby community of Uncertain has an eclectic charm you might want to explore. There are interesting nooks and crannies worth seeking out if you decide on a side trip there, which will add five miles each way from the park to your bike ride.

The return to Jefferson from the park also travels through thick forests, but along roads that carry more traffic than the peaceful trail through the park. Back in Jefferson, there are all sorts of things to do and see, including more bike riding to the west along the **Lake O' the Pines Ramble.**

The Basics

Start: In front of the Marion County courthouse on Polk St., also named FM 2208 and Business 59. There is parking throughout the restored downtown historic district, on side streets, and in public lots. Jefferson is on US 59 about 10 miles north of I–20, about 160 miles east of Dallas and 60 miles west of Shreveport, Louisiana.
Distance: 33.5 miles.
Terrain: Rolling hills.
Roads: Traffic increases on the return from Caddo Lake State Park. There is an adequate shoulder on Texas 43, but the shoulder comes and goes on Texas 49, which has heavier traffic closer to Jefferson. Other roads are two lanes, light traffic.

Food: Lots of options in Jefferson; convenience stores near Caddo Lake State Park.

Miles & Directions

- 0.0 Start on Polk St. in front of courthouse. Head south away from downtown over the bayou. Adequate shoulder along busy street.
- 1.0 Bear left (south) onto FM 134, following sign to Karnack as FM 2208 veers right. Two lanes, no shoulder, undulating terrain. Trees are cleared back for pastures.
- 4.1 Cross Little Cypress Bayou.
- 8.9 Cross railroad tracks.
- 9.9 Cross Hagerty Creek, past creek and swampland.
- 12.1 Pass convenience store.
- 12.4 Stop sign intersection with Texas 43. Continue across to the park. After crossing Texas 43 the road becomes FM 2198 (east).
- 12.9 Turn left onto Park Rd. 2 and enter Caddo Lake State Park.
- 13.0 Pass park ranger station. The short park road is a fabulous trail—narrow, thickly wooded up to the road, twisty, and steep.
- 15.2 Exit the park and turn right, back onto FM 2198 (west).

FM 2198 east continues into the town of Uncertain and the shore of Caddo Lake in 4.5 miles. There are stores and restaurants there, as well as some neighborhood side streets to explore.

- 15.7 Turn right (north) onto Texas 43. Two lanes with traffic and an adequate shoulder.
- 16.9 Long crossing (0.5 mile) of Big Cypress Bayou, where shoulder narrows over bridge.
- 20.1 Pass junction of FM 805 (east) to the right. Don't take this turn.
- 20.3 Turn left (west) onto FM 805, marked as the Texas Forest Trail, carefully crossing traffic lanes. Two lanes, no shoulder.
- 24.6 Turn left (west) onto Texas 49 at stop sign T intersection.

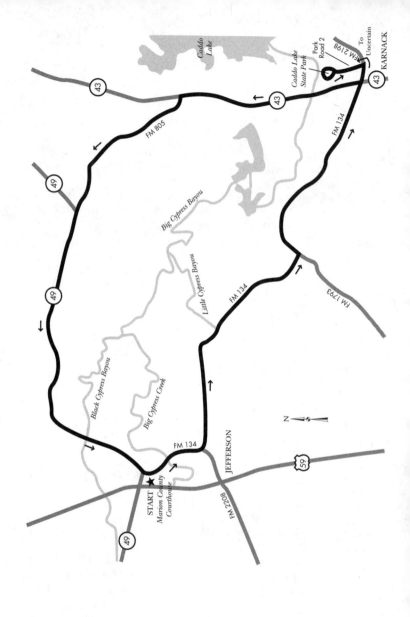

Shoulder comes and goes throughout this portion of route. Hilly here, with several bayou crossings.

- 31.0 Cross Black Cypress Bayou.
- 31.7 Pass Jefferson town sign.
- 32.6 Cross railroad tracks.
- 33.0 Turn left (south) onto FM 134 at busy junction. This is downtown, also called Polk St. Traffic thickens but slows as it enters historic district of downtown.
- 33.5 Finish at Marion County courthouse.

24

Lake O' the Pines Ramble

Jefferson—Lake O' the Pines—Kellyville—Jefferson

This is the second of two rides starting from the shore of Big Cypress Bayou in the charming town of Jefferson. This route heads west from Jefferson, passing through terrain quite different from that encountered on rides to the east. There's none of the swampy, bayou-filled countryside characteristic of the **Caddo Lake Cruise** here. Instead, this route passes over rolling countryside cleared of forests for farms and pastures toward the Lake O' the Pines.

The Lake O' the Pines is the result of a U.S. Army Corps of Engineers flood-control project in the Red River Basin. It's among the most popular lake recreation areas in east Texas and is especially prized by bass fishermen. You'll have a good view of the lake as you ride for more than two miles along the Ferrells Bridge Dam, which impounds the lake on its eastern border.

A historical marker near the beginning of this route recounts the development of some of the roads you'll travel on your way toward Lake O' the Pines. The overland routes to Jefferson began as traces, narrow footpaths used by Indians to mark their way through the wilderness. Traces later became boundaries by which surveyors mapped early land grants and served as reference points to guide immigrants into the Texas territories. Accessible by trace roads and deep-water navigation, the Jefferson area was well known to travelers and settlers before a town was actually laid out in the 1840s.

Parts of the countryside west of Jefferson are composed of iron-rich siltstones and sandstones and are known to geologists as the Weches formation. These ore deposits supported some of the earliest iron and steel foundries in Texas. A foundry in the community of Kellyville, which you'll pass on the return to Jefferson after crossing the lake dam, was a major producer of plows and farm implements for settlers heading west through this area after the Civil War.

Since this route shares its starting point with the **Caddo Lake Cruise**, you can combine the two rides for sixty miles of cycling between these two very different lakes.

The Basics

Start: In front of the Marion County courthouse on Polk St., also named FM 2208 and Business 59. There is parking throughout the restored downtown historic district, on side streets, and in public lots. Jefferson is on US 59 about 10 miles north of I–20, 160 miles east of Dallas, and 60 miles west of Shreveport, Louisiana.

Distance: 26.5 miles.

Terrain: Gently rolling hills, a little steeper leaving the dam across the lake.

Roads: Traffic leaving from and returning to town. FM roads are two lanes, no shoulder, with lighter traffic after crossing US 59. Texas 49 on the return has high-speed traffic but a shoulder.

Food: Only at the start in Jefferson.

Miles & Directions

- 0.0 Start on Polk St. in front of courthouse. Head south away from downtown over the bayou. Adequate shoulder along busy street.
- 1.0 Stay right (south) on FM 2208 as FM 134 diverges to the left. Pass historical marker (mile 1.7) for Trammel's Trace.
- 2.1 Carefully cross four lanes of US 59.
- 2.4 Cross railroad tracks. Road is fairly flat, two lanes, no shoulder, trees cut back for fields.
- 8.2 Turn right (west) onto FM 3001. Same character of road, passing several trailer homes.

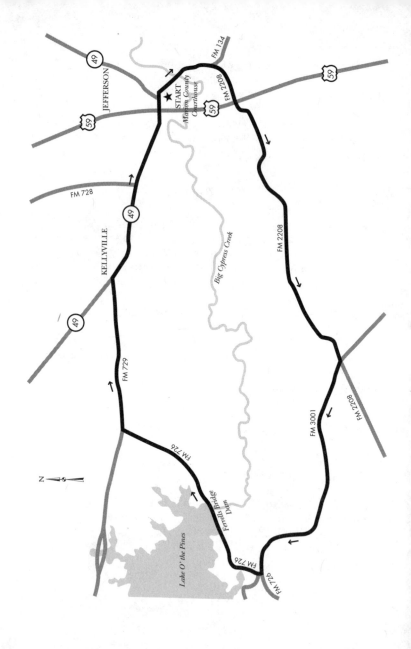

- 13.9 Turn right (east) onto FM 726 and immediately enter Lake O' the Pines (there's a sign here). Two lanes, no shoulder, and a guardrail, along Ferrells Bridge Dam for about 2 miles, past two access roads to shore and dam spillway.
- 16.1 After crossing the dam there are some steeper rolling sections in the road.
- 18.8 Turn right (east) onto FM 729 at stop sign T intersection. Wide shoulder becomes a climbing lane from time to time.
- 22.2 Turn right (east) onto Texas 49. Mostly wide shoulder.
- 25.0 Pass Jefferson town sign, shoulder ends.
- 25.6 Cross railroad tracks.
- 26.0 Turn right (south) onto FM 134 at busy intersection. This is Polk St. going through restored downtown.
- 26.5 Finish in front of Marion County courthouse.

Tyler Rose Classic

Tyler—Chandler—Brownsboro—
Murchison—Edom—Tyler

Roses are Tyler's trademark. Each spring, Tyler and all of east Texas show off colorful redbuds, dogwoods, azaleas, and wildflowers. Throughout the year, visitors to Tyler can also find some type of rose in bloom.

This ride starts on the west side of Tyler at the Tyler Rose Garden, which houses a rose museum, rose library, and the country's largest municipal rose garden. More than one-fifth of the commercial rose bushes in America are grown in the Tyler area, and roses are celebrated here in more ways than you can imagine.

Tyler is a large city, and there is heavy traffic on roads without shoulders for the first and last four miles of this route. These roads do have wide lanes with some room for cars to pass, and there are signs on these busy thoroughfares warning of the presence of bicycles. Motorists see their share of cyclists on these roads, especially during the popular Beauty and the Beast bicycle tour. The course laid out here travels west of Tyler along some of the roads used in past editions of the Beauty and the Beast ride.

This tour travels west on Texas 31 to the town of Chandler, then turns south toward Lake Palestine. If you'd rather miss the traffic on Texas 31 altogether, consider starting your ride in Chandler. As the course continues west from Chandler, traffic gradually lessens, and the countryside becomes increasingly peaceful.

After crossing a long causeway over Lake Palestine, there are two distance options to choose from. Each passes in and out of pleasant pastureland and wooded areas, with more challenging terrain on the longer route. You'll travel through several small agricultural communities along the way, where roadside stands selling Noonday onions and Tyler roses are plentiful.

On the return to Tyler, there is an option to avoid a short stretch that adds a half-mile hill climb to your ride. This hill is the "Beast" of the Beauty and the Beast route, difficult only because it comes after so many miles of cycling. The roads up to and over the "Beast" continue through pleasant countryside, displaying more of the beauty of this part of east Texas before your ride connects with the busy roads back to the Tyler Rose Garden.

The Basics

Start: At the Tyler Rose Garden on the corner of Texas 31 (also called W. Front St.) and Rose Park Dr. in front of the Harvey Convention Center. There's a lot of parking behind the convention center by the Rose Garden Center and Rose Museum.

Distance: 71.0 miles or 52.3 miles. Both routes can be shortened by 5.7 miles at Texas 64. To encounter minimal traffic, start in Chandler rather than Tyler for routes of 48.8 miles or 30.1 miles.

Terrain: Gently rolling terrain, a little more pronounced on the longer option. One long climb toward the end of each route, which can be avoided by shortening the ride by 5.7 miles.

Roads: Heavy traffic on Texas 31 and Texas 64. Some traffic on FM

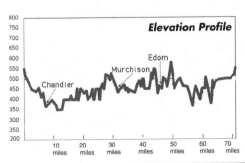

137

315 south of Chandler. Other roads are two lanes, no shoulder, light traffic.

Food: Several options in Tyler and Chandler; convenience store after crossing Lake Palestine; stores in Brownsboro (shorter option), Murchison, and Edom.

Miles & Directions

- 0.0 Exit the Rose Garden by turning left (west) onto Texas 31/ W. Front St. Four lanes, no shoulder, traffic.
- 1.1 Continue straight through the stoplight at Loop 323 as the road becomes six lanes. Signs mark this as a bike route.
- 4.0 Pick up a wide shoulder as you pass intersection with FM 206.
- 8.1 Cross Neches River.
- 8.4 Pass Chandler town sign
- 8.9 Lose shoulder in town.
- 9.2 Pass convenience stores.
- 9.8 At stoplight, turn left onto FM 315, also called Broad St. Two lanes, no shoulder.

To avoid the traffic on Texas 31, you can begin your ride from this intersection. See directions to return to this point from mile 55.0 of the full tour.

- 9.9 Cross railroad tracks.
- 11.3 Pass Chandler town sign.
- 11.5 Pick up shoulder as you cross Lake Palestine.
- 12.8 Complete crossing of Lake Palestine and lose shoulder.
- 13.0 Pass a convenience store and the intersection of FM 3079 to the right.

For a shorter option totaling 52.3 miles, turn right onto FM 3079. After 5.2 miles, at a stop sign, turn right (north) onto FM 314. After 9.8 miles and the intersection with Texas 31, continue straight on FM 314 past a convenience store and across railroad tracks. After

14.9 miles turn right at a stop sign onto FM 279. There is a convenience store here. From this point follow the directions for the full tour from mile 46.6 to return to Tyler.

- 14.3 Turn right (west) onto FM 317.
- 18.0 Continue straight on FM 317 across FM 314 at stop sign intersection.
- 23.1 Pass a convenience store and FM 607 to the right.
- 26.4 Turn right (north) onto FM 1803.
- 30.2 Carefully turn left across traffic onto Texas 31. Two lanes, shoulder.
- 31.7 Pass Murchison town sign.
- 32.4 Pass a convenience store and turn right (north) onto FM 773.
- 32.5 Cross railroad tracks.
- 36.8 Cross Kickapoo Creek.
- 38.3 Continue straight past FM 1803 to the right.
- 38.8 Enter VanZandt County.
- 39.3 Turn right (east) on FM 2339 toward Edom, into wooded terrain and more subtle hills.
- 45.4 Pass Edom town sign.
- 46.3 At stop sign T intersection, bear right onto FM 279, following signs to Tyler.
- 46.6 Continue straight on FM 279 past the FM 314 intersection. There is a convenience store and the shorter option rejoins here.
- 47.2 Pass another convenience store.
- 53.4 Continue straight past the intersection of FM 2010 to right.
- 55.0 Continue straight past the junction of FM 315 to the right.

By turning right onto FM 315 here, you'll come to the stoplight intersection with Texas 31 in Chandler (mile 9.8 of the full tour) after 3.6 miles.

- 56.4 After passing over a road built up to cross boggy countryside and crossing a bridge, enter Smith County.

- 57.3 Turn left (west) on Texas 64; two lanes, wide shoulder.

To shorten the ride by 5.7 miles and eliminate a large hill, turn right on Texas 64. After 2.2 miles, pass the intersection with FM 724 on the left and follow the directions for the full tour from mile 65.2 by continuing straight on Texas 64 to return to Tyler.

- 58.8 Turn right following sign to New Harmony onto County Rd. 413.
- 60.8 Turn right at unmarked T intersection with FM 724 (New Harmony to left).
- 62.6 Begin climb of 0.4 mile (this hill is the "Beast" in the Beauty and the Beast ride).
- 65.2 Turn left (east) onto Texas 64; four lanes, no shoulder.
- 67.6 Turn right onto Patton La., also marked as County Rd. 1155. This turn is easy to miss; it's the next street after Eisenhower Rd., which is better marked.
- 68.7 At stop sign, turn left carefully across traffic onto Texas 31.
- 69.9 Continue straight through the stoplight intersection with Loop 323.
- 71.0 Finish at Tyler Rose Garden.

26

Palestine Challenge

Palestine—Elmwood—Brushy Creek—
Pert—Neches—Palestine

Palestine is a historic east Texas town in a very pretty setting. Flowering dogwoods and wildflowers in spring and fall foliage in autumn add bright, beautiful colors to the Piney Woods here.

Quiet county roads cross the forests and meadows around Palestine. For more than fifty years, visitors each spring have come to explore these roads during Palestine's annual Texas Dogwood Trails celebration. Recently, the chamber of commerce has promoted a fall cycling tour along some of these roads. A ride along these roads is especially attractive during the change of seasons, but it can be enjoyed any time of the year.

There are pretty roads and places of interest in all directions from Palestine. The western terminus for the Texas State Railroad is a nice state park on the eastern edge of Palestine, about twenty-five miles from the start of the **Texas State Railroad Challenge** in Rusk. There are more good roads to ride south and east in the direction of the Davy Crockett National Forest, toward the area of the **El Camino Real Challenge.** A course over equally attractive but less well-known roads to the north of Palestine is set out for you here.

The highlights of this tour are the stretches that travel over Anderson County roads. These narrow, secluded lanes pass through forests and fields in some of the area's smaller farming communities. Leaving from the Anderson County courthouse, the route passes Davy Dogwood Park, which has an unusually thick growth of dogwood trees, and immediately turns onto an eight-mile stretch of county road. This county road is often twisted and hilly, with trees lining the edge of the road for much of the way.

After connecting with FM roads, a shorter option is available to loop back to Palestine. The full tour continues further north along roads marked as the Texas Forest Trail toward the Brushy Creek community. Just past the store at Brushy Creek, the route follows another Anderson County road for several miles, eventually connecting with FM roads to Neches. The return from Neches follows busier roads back to the courthouse in Palestine.

The Basics

Start: At the Anderson County courthouse in Palestine. There is public parking around the courthouse and on side streets throughout downtown. Palestine is about 50 miles southwest of Tyler.
Distance: 50.2 miles or 23.8 miles.
Terrain: Hilly and forested.
Roads: Anderson County roads are one lane with some rough surfaces, lightly traveled. FM roads are two lanes, no shoulders, with some traffic on the return to Palestine on FM 3309. There are unregulated crossings of Texas 155 and US 79, which have four lanes and high-speed traffic.
Food: Many choices in Palestine; store in Brushy Creek; store in Neches 0.2 mile from the route.

Miles & Directions

- 0.0 Leave the Anderson County courthouse and head north on Texas 19 (also called N. Church) from the corner of E. Lacy and N. Church.
- 0.4 Carefully turn left (south) across traffic onto US 79. Four lanes, no shoulder.
- 0.6 At traffic light turn right onto Texas 155. Four lanes, no shoulder.

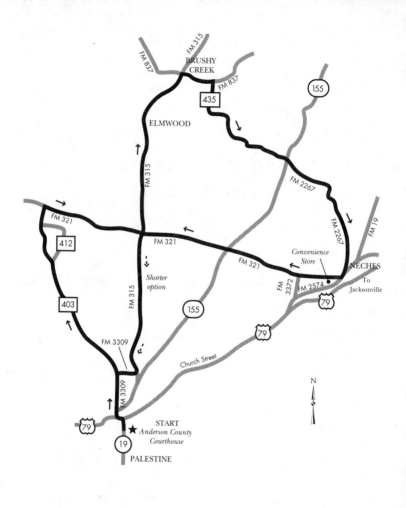

- 0.8 Pass post office and turn left (north) onto N. Link St./FM 3309. Two wide lanes, no shoulder.
- 1.4 Continue straight through stop sign junction with Loop 256, following sign for Dogwood Trails.
- 1.9 Pass Davy Dogwood Park on left.
- 2.3 Stay straight onto Anderson County Rd. 403 as FM 3309 bends sharply to the right. Several Anderson County roads will merge along the way. Anderson County Rd. 403 bears to the left and intersections are poorly marked. Road surfaces are rough in spots.
- 2.7 Pass Anderson County Rd. 404 to left and encounter more rolling hills.
- 7.4 Bear left at Y intersection with Anderson County Rd. 412.
- 8.1 Bear left at unmarked Y intersection.
- 8.8 Reconnect with Anderson County Rd. 412 again. Continue to bear left.
- 9.5 Continue straight past Anderson County Rd. 414.
- 10.2 At unmarked stop sign T intersection, turn right onto FM 321. Two lanes, no shoulder, light traffic, and a sign directing bike route to the right. Terrain becomes hillier, with long climbs and views into surrounding countryside.
- 15.4 At stop sign, turn left onto FM 315, marked as the Texas Forest Trail, toward the Brushy Creek community.

For a shorter option totaling 23.8 miles, turn right here and follow the directions for the full tour from mile 41.8 to return to Palestine.

- 16.2 Cross Mound Prairie Creek toward more open pastureland.
- 18.3 Pass Elmwood town sign.
- 21.8 Pass Brushy Creek town sign.
- 22.0 At stop sign, turn right onto FM 837 toward Frankston. Brushy Creek store is on the corner. Two lanes, no shoulder, light traffic.
- 23.9 Turn right onto Anderson County Rd. 435. This turn comes up quickly and is not well marked. Though a one-lane road with a rough surface at first, this is a nice country lane.
- 28.5 Continue straight at stop sign intersection with Texas 155;

cross busy road carefully. After crossing, road becomes FM 2267 (east); two lanes, no shoulder.

- 33.8 Turn right (west) onto FM 321 in Neches.

There is a store 0.2 mile away. Turn left here, then in 50 yards turn right onto FM 2574 toward Cannon's convenience store.

- 38.3 At stop sign, carefully cross Texas 155 and continue straight on FM 321.
- 41.8 Turn left (south) onto FM 315 toward town. Rolling hills, some traffic. The shorter option rejoins here.
- 47.1 Turn right (south) onto FM 3309.
- 47.9 At stop sign, FM 3309 bears hard left at junction with Anderson County Rd. 403 and becomes N. Link St. Turn left.
- 48.9 Continue straight through stoplight at Loop 256 junction.
- 49.5 Turn right onto Texas 155.
- 49.7 Turn left onto US 79/Texas 155 at stoplight.
- 49.8 Turn right onto Texas 19/Mallard St.
- 50.2 Turn west on Lacy and go 1 block to finish at Anderson County courthouse.

27

Texas State Railroad Challenge

Rusk—Dialville—Union Grove—Lake Jacksonville—
Pierces Chapel—Maydelle—Rusk

This bike ride starts at the Texas State Railroad depot in Rusk. The route heads north and west through the forests and rural communities of Cherokee County, over some challenging hills, and along a lovely lakeshore.

Cherokee Indians made their home in this part of Texas in the early nineteenth century after being pushed out of the southeast United States. The Mexican government welcomed the Cherokees into their Texas territory, hoping their presence would deter illegal immigration from the new American states. Neither the Mexican government nor the founders of the Texas Republic after them made good on promises to give the Cherokees title to the land they occupied. Instead, by 1839, an army of the Texas Republic had driven all the Cherokees north into Arkansas. The county name is a tribute to these Indians' brief presence here.

Rusk is the seat of Cherokee County, and there are lovely parks throughout town. One park includes the state's longest footbridge, built in the 1860s, to enable residents to get from one side of town to the other in wet weather. Instead of starting in town, though, this ride begins at the beautifully restored railroad depot in Rusk State Park on the west side of town.

A local railroad line was built from Rusk more than one hundred years ago to haul the wood that fueled the foundry in the town's prison. The rail line was connected to Palestine early in the twentieth century but was subsequently leased out or unused until the state took it over in 1972.

Today the railroad line is a unit of the Texas Parks and Wildlife Department, which operates antique steam engine trains over the track between Rusk and Palestine. The train provides a fun ride along an attractive route through thick woods and over scenic creeks. This bike route parallels a small portion of the train's path on its return along US 84.

The bike route set out here heads west from the park through the communities of Dialville and Union Grove. The farmland and pastureland it passes through becomes increasingly forested. By the time the route turns north toward Lake Jacksonville, you'll feel as if you're deep in the woods. The county roads around the lake are particularly pretty, with vacation homes tucked away on some of the side roads accessing the lake. These county roads are twisted and nicely shaded, with trees coming right up to the curb on several stretches.

After passing the lake, the route turns south along the very hilly FM 747, which is thick with trees displaying nice colors in the fall. At the bottom of this lovely stretch is the I. D. Fairchild State Forest, once the site of a state sawmill but rebuilt by the Civilian Conservation Corps during the Depression and preserved today as a wildlife sanctuary. The return to Rusk along US 84, a busy road with a wide shoulder, parallels portions of the route of the Texas State Railroad. Along the way you'll pass historical markers recounting some of the Indian heritage of Cherokee County before finishing at the train depot on the west side of Rusk.

The Basics

Start: Rusk State Park, on US 84. There may be a fee to park, and there is a fare to ride the train. Rusk is about 50 miles south of Tyler.

Distance: 38.7 miles or 21.7 miles.

Terrain: Extremely hilly, especially on FM 747.
Roads: US 84 has a wide shoulder, or climbing lane; other roads are lightly traveled.
Food: Concessions in Rusk State Park; stores in Maydelle.

Miles & Directions

- 0.0 Exit park at Park Rd. 76 intersection by turning left (west) onto US 84; two lanes, high-speed traffic, 6-foot shoulder. Train terminal is 0.5 mile from this intersection on the Park Rd.
- 1.4 Pass Oakland town sign.
- 1.6 Turn right (north) onto FM 347. Two lanes, no shoulder through the Oakland community and surrounding pastureland.
- 4.6 Bear left at Y intersection to stay on FM 347.
- 5.1 After entering Dialville, turn left (west) onto FM 1910, near a historical marker describing settlement in 1822.
- 9.8 Turn right (north) onto FM 2138, past the Union Grove community.

For a shorter option totaling 21.7 miles, turn left (south) onto FM 2138, a stretch with some steep descents. After 5.3 miles, carefully turn left across traffic at the stop sign T intersection in Maydelle onto US 84. There are two convenience stores here. Follow directions for the full tour from mile 32.1 to return to Rusk.

- 10.7 Bear left onto South Shore Dr./County Rd. 3108, a fabulous, narrow road passing along the border of Lake Jacksonville. Immediately thereafter, bear right at the Y intersection with Sheffield Rd. to stay on this county road, which is mismarked as CR 3109. Very twisted, thickly wooded, short hills in some places. You'll pass many other intersections of county roads; stay on the main road all the way.
- 15.4 Bear right onto County Rd. 3111.
- 16.0 At Y intersection, turn hard left (south) onto FM 747. There are no stores in the nearby community of New Hope to

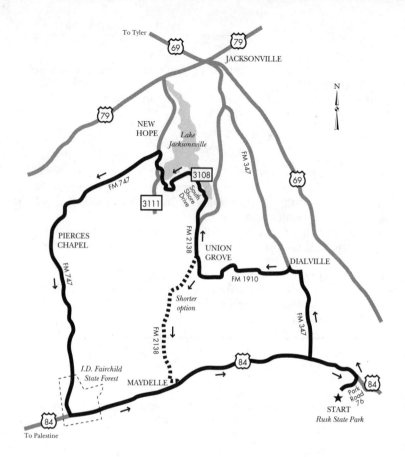

the right. FM 747 is a very hilly, beautiful stretch with thick foliage and terrific fall colors.

- 21.1 Enter the community of Pierces Chapel.
- 28.1 At stop sign T intersection, carefully turn left (east) onto US 84. At this intersection is the I. D. Fairchild State Forest, which has a historical marker recounting its early history as a state sawmill and Civilian Conservation Corps camp. Now a wildlife sanctuary, it is especially beautiful. Wide shoulder on US 84 unless it becomes a climbing lane.
- 32.1 Pass Maydelle, with two convenience stores. The shorter option rejoins here.
- 37.1 Pass Dialville and intersection of FM 347, just past historical marker describing settlement of Little Bean's Cherokee Village.
- 38.7 Finish at Rusk State Park.

28

El Camino Real Challenge

---

*Alto—Caddoan Mounds State Historical Park—
Weches—Mission Tejas State Historical Park—
Augusta—Percilla—Alto*

Texas 21 through east Texas was once El Camino Real, the "Royal Road" traveled by Spanish missionaries and explorers throughout their "new world" from Florida to Mexico. Indians native to east Texas used these same pathways centuries before the Spanish arrived. A bike ride along these oldest of Texas roads passes some fascinating remains of the early Spanish and Indian inhabitants.

The starting point for this ride is Alto, just south of Rusk and the **Texas State Railroad Challenge.** This small town began as a Spanish outpost on El Camino Real at the point perceived to be the highest, or *mas alto,* between the Neches and Angelina rivers. Look for parking along the side streets near the starting point of this route or in one of the many church parking lots near the center of town.

Texas 21 leaving Alto is lined with historical markers and plaques denoting points of interest along the route of El Camino Real. The route begins through fairly unassuming pastureland, but after six miles it comes to the Caddoan Mounds State Historical Park. Through archeological excavations and preserved burial mounds, the park tells some of the story of the great Indian cultures that inhabited this area from prehistoric times. You'll notice the influence of the Caddoan Indians in Texas in place names along other routes in this book, from the **Caddo Lake Cruise** near

Jefferson in east Texas, to the Caddo community on the **Possum Kingdom Challenge** west of Fort Worth.

A mile past the Caddoan mounds, the character of the course changes dramatically as it enters the Davy Crockett National Forest. The ride now is through thick woods and over creek and river crossings on the way to Mission Tejas State Historical Park, site of the first Spanish mission in east Texas. A historical marker at this pretty park describes the establishment of Mission San Francisco de los Tejas here in 1690 in response to the threat of unsuccessful French expeditions a few years earlier. The park rangers are used to seeing cyclists, and you may be able to get your water bottles filled here in a pinch.

The return to Alto continues along largely tree-lined roads that are just north of the boundary of the Davy Crockett National Forest. As there are no opportunities to stop for food on the way back, a shorter distance option is included. Be sure your water bottles are filled in Weches or at the Mission Tejas park.

The Basics

Start: In Alto, at the intersection where US 69, Texas 294, and Texas 21 converge. Look for parking on nearby side streets or in the many church parking lots. Alto is 25 miles west of Nacogdoches on Texas 21.

Distance: 49.0 miles or 40.4 miles.

Terrain: Gently rolling terrain, some flat stretches.

Roads: All roads are two lanes, no shoulder. Traffic on Texas 21 and Texas 294 is higher speed.

Food: Options in Alto; convenience store in Weches.

Miles & Directions

- 0.0 From the intersection with US 69, head west on Texas 21/294 through the town center.
- 0.2 Bear left to stay on Texas 21 where it diverges from Texas

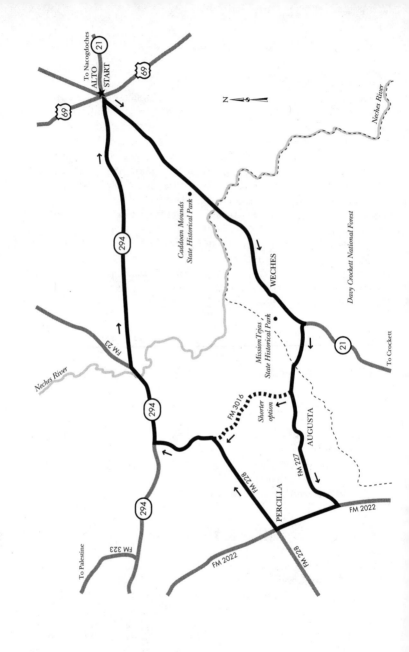

294, following signs directing you toward Crockett and Caddoan Mounds State Historical Park. Two-lane road, some shoulder from time to time.

- 6.0 Pass Caddoan Mounds State Historical Park on the right.
- 6.2 Pass Mound Prairie historical marker describing the Caddoan Indian settlements here.
- 6.7 Pretty descent through a corridor of trees toward Neches River. Character of the land changes as you enter Davy Crockett National Forest: more forests, some bogs, hillier.
- 12.1 Pass Weches town sign.
- 12.3 Pass convenience store.
- 12.6 Park Rd. 44 marking Mission Tejas State Historical Park to the right.
- 14.0 Turn right (west) onto FM 227, through countryside filled with trees and pastures. Two lanes, no shoulder, less traffic.
- 17.2 Continue straight (west) on FM 227 past the intersection with FM 3016.

For a shorter option totaling 40.4 miles, turn right (north) onto FM 3016, marked as the Texas Forest Trail. After 4.5 miles, at the stop sign T intersection, turn right onto FM 228. Follow the instructions for the full tour from mile 30.3 to return to Alto.

- 19.5 Pass through the Augusta community.
- 22.9 Turn right (north) onto FM 2022.
- 25.8 Turn right (east) onto FM 228 through the community of Percilla.
- 30.3 Continue straight on FM 228 past the intersection with FM 3016. The shorter option rejoins here.
- 33.2 Turn right (east) onto Texas 294, through some pretty forest. Extremely hilly, no shoulder, higher-speed traffic similar to Texas 21.
- 36.1 Cross Neches River.
- 48.8 Turn left (east) back toward Alto at the intersection with Texas 21.
- 49.0 Finish in Alto.

29

San Augustine Cruise

San Augustine—Angelina National Forest—
Chireno—San Augustine

Further east on El Camino Real between two national forests and two large reservoirs sits the town of San Augustine. The town grew around a Spanish mission settled along the Spanish road in the early 1700s close to French outposts in nearby Louisiana.

Only thirty miles from the Louisiana border, San Augustine was a principal crossing point into Texas for early settlers. Sam Houston, Davy Crockett, and other prominent figures in the history of the Republic entered Texas along El Camino Real and the old San Antonio Road through San Augustine.

San Augustine today attracts visitors to the outdoors, principally for fishing in the Sam Rayburn or Toledo Bend reservoirs and for camping and hiking in the Angelina and Sabine National Forests. The roads through these remote areas are also pleasant places to cycle.

This route travels through the countryside south and west of San Augustine. A few miles after leaving San Augustine, the route skirts the northern border of the Angelina National Forest, the smallest of the four national forests in the Piney Woods area of east Texas. A shorter option turns north and joins El Camino Real near the town of Chireno. The full tour continues west through the national forest and crosses the northern edge of the Sam Rayburn Reservoir near the Attoyac Bayou.

Past the bayou the route heads north into Chireno, a small

community on the path of El Camino Real. There are a café and stores in Chireno where you can rest or resupply for the remainder of your ride. From Chireno the route returns to San Augustine along Texas 21.

This ride is in a remote, rural east Texas setting. San Augustine is a small town with limited options for accommodations if you're not camping nearby. Nacogdoches to the west and Center to the north are larger towns of interest and make good bases for exploring this area.

The Basics

Start: At the traffic circle intersection of Texas 21 and US 96 in San Augustine. There is public parking at the chamber of commerce located 0.4 mile from the traffic circle on Texas 21 east. San Augustine is about 120 miles north of Beaumont.

Distance: 41.2 miles or 31.4 miles.

Terrain: Rolling hills.

Roads: Roads and shoulders further east in Texas are narrower than usual. Texas 103 (used for 2.9 miles) has high-speed traffic and a wide shoulder. Texas 21 has some traffic as well. Other roads are relatively quiet, two-lane roads.

Food: Several choices in San Augustine and Chireno.

Miles & Directions

- 0.0 From traffic circle intersection of Texas 21 and US 96, head south on US 96.
- 0.1 Turn right (south) onto FM 1277, also named Partin Rd. here. Two lanes, no shoulder.
- 2.9 Pass Spur 85 to the right.
- 13.7 Continue past FM 1196 intersection.

For a shorter ride totaling 31.2 miles, turn right (north) onto FM 1196. After 6.9 miles, at a stop sign T intersection, turn right onto

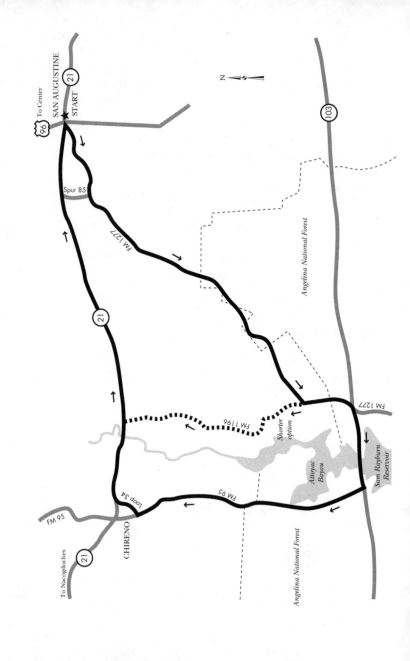

Texas 21 and follow directions for the full tour from mile 30.6 to return to San Augustine. If you need supplies, Collard's Country Store is 1.1 miles to the left of this intersection in Chireno.

- 15.5 Turn right (west) onto Texas 103. High-speed traffic and wide shoulder.
- 18.0 Cross 0.5-mile bridge over portion of Sam Rayburn Reservoir/Attoyac Bayou.
- 18.4 Turn right (north) onto FM 95 through the Angelina National Forest.
- 25.8 Pass Chireno town sign.
- 27.0 Stores and café in center of Chireno. Turn right and downhill at the caution light onto Loop 34.
- 27.8 At the stop sign T intersection, turn right (east) onto Texas 21. Wide shoulder, two lanes.
- 30.6 Pass intersection with FM 1196 to the right. The shorter option rejoins here.
- 33.8 Pass town sign for the Denning community. Texas 21 here is marked as the Texas Forest Trail.
- 38.9 Pass Spur 85 to the right.
- 41.2 Finish at traffic circle in San Augustine.

Southeast Texas
and the Gulf Coast

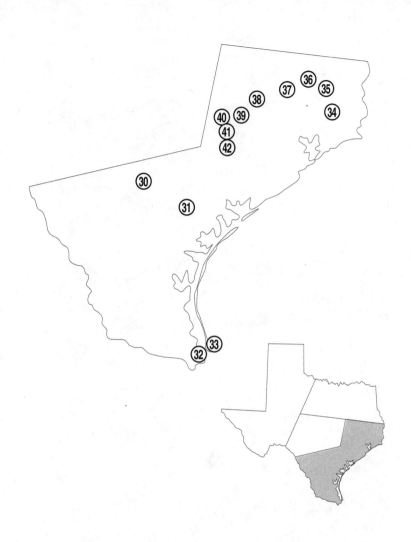

Southeast Texas and the Gulf Coast

30

San Antonio Missions Ramble

Missions Concepción—San José—San Juan—Espada

The city of San Antonio grew up around five Spanish missions established along the San Antonio River in the early 1700s. Almost three hundred years after their founding, the missions remain beautifully preserved and located in the heart of one of America's largest and most distinctive cities.

Four of these missions are administered by the National Park Service as the San Antonio Missions National Historical Park. The fifth, Mission San Antonio de Valero, is known to Texans as the Alamo. You can visit the Alamo in the heart of San Antonio, just three miles north of the start of this Ramble.

All five missions are unique cultural, as well as historical, resources for the people of San Antonio. The four missions in the National Park maintain active parishes under the auspices of the Archdiocese of San Antonio. Visitors to Mission San José, the largest and best-known of the park missions, are welcome to enjoy the lively music of the "mariachi mass" held each Sunday. The architecture of the missions, combining traditional Spanish design with the influences of Mexican builders, is further evidence of San Antonio's rich heritage.

A well-marked route along neighborhood and park roads connects the four missions in the National Park. While cycling this route, you can stop to visit any or all of these four missions, along with parts of the original irrigation system designed to support the

164

life of the mission settlements. The Espada Dam and the Espada Aqueduct still divert water to nearby properties for irrigation.

On most Saturday mornings, park rangers lead a guided bicycle tour of portions of the park, leaving from Mission San José. This tour covers about ten miles and lasts about three hours. Mark Tenzel is one of the knowledgeable and dedicated rangers involved in this special way to explore the missions trail. Call ahead (210–229–4470) for more information and to make arrangements to take advantage of this unique opportunity.

The tour set out here leaves from Mission Concepción at the north end of the park. The route briefly heads south on a well-traveled city street before turning onto a quieter park road. In the park you'll notice stretches of paved hike-and-bike trails. These trails are usually fine to use, but from time to time they are under repair or construction. As a result, this ride stays on local streets throughout its course.

The ride continues through Espada Park, over the Espada Dam, and past Mission San Juan. Continuing on to Mission Espada, the route follows the narrow Camino Coahuilteca (pronounced kwaweel-tekens), named for the local Indians originally ministered to at the missions. There is a nice crossing of the San Antonio River, the thread that connects all of San Antonio's missions, on the camino.

Past Mission Espada, the route turns north toward Mission San José along busier city roads. Mission Road on this part of the route contains one unregulated crossing of a busy six-lane road. If you are uncomfortable with a busy traffic crossing, follow the option to retrace your steps from Mission San Juan through the park road over the Espada Dam. If you take this route, don't pass up a side trip to Mission San José, perhaps the most significant of the missions in the National Park.

The Basics

Start: In San Antonio at Mission Concepción, located about 3 miles south of downtown San Antonio. Follow St. Mary's St. south from downtown until it becomes Mission Rd.

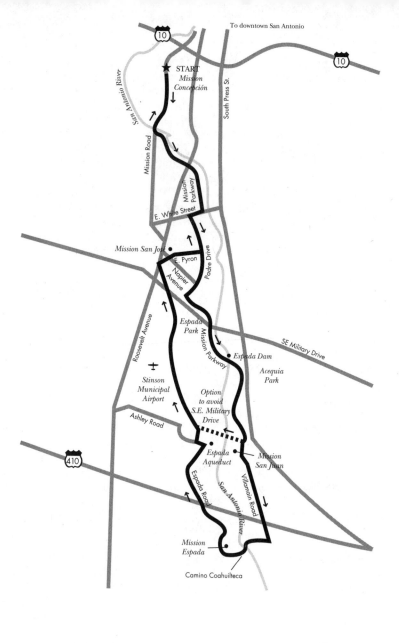

Distance: 14.3 miles.
Terrain: Flat.
Roads: Traffic on Mission Rd., which has some rough surfaces. Mission Pkwy., Padre, Villamain, and Camino Coahuilteca are lightly traveled.
Food: Vending machines at Mission San José, some stores near Mission Concepción.

Miles & Directions

- 0.0 Leaving Mission Concepción, head south on Mission Rd., past the Riverside Golf Course on the left. Two lanes, no shoulder, some traffic, rough surface.
- 0.7 Cross bridge over San Antonio River.
- 0.8 Turn left onto Mission Pkwy., following sign to Mission San José. Nice road with less traffic through park.
- 2.0 Turn right briefly onto E. White St., a busy street.
- 2.1 Turn left onto Padre; less traffic past Mission County Park.
- 2.8 Continue straight past the intersection with E. Pyron St. You can see Mission San José at the end of E. Pyron 0.4 mile to the right.
- 2.9 Continue straight on Padre past the intersection with Napier on the right, onto a nice park road.
- 3.6 Enter Espada Park.
- 4.1 Carefully cross low-water spillway at Espada Dam and continue through Acequia Park. Note hike-and-bike trail with old wooden bridges through the park.
- 5.3 At stop sign intersection, continue straight toward Mission San Juan.
- 5.5 Pass entrance to Mission San Juan.
- 5.6 Turn right at stop sign onto Villamain, following sign to Mission Espada; two lanes, no shoulder, light traffic.
- 6.4 Pass under I–410 underpass.
- 6.5 Turn right onto Camino Coahuilteca, a nice country lane with a water crossing.
- 7.0 Pass Mission Espada entrance.

- 7.1 Turn right onto Espada; two lanes, light traffic.
- 8.5 Turn left toward Ashley Rd. (unmarked) at the Espada Aqueduct, following sign for Mission San José.
- 8.6 A quick right turn onto another unmarked road, which is still Ashley Rd.
- 8.9 At the stop sign, turn left onto Mission Rd. (unmarked).

About 1.5 miles from this point, there will be an unregulated crossing of a 6-lane road with heavy traffic. You can avoid this busy intersection by turning right here. After 0.4 mile you'll come to a stop sign intersection with Padre at the entrance to Acequia Park (mile 5.3 of the full tour). By turning left here, you can retrace your steps to return to Mission Concepción. You can reach Mission San José by turning left onto Napier or E. Pyron after you exit Acequia Park.

- 9.3 Pass entrance to Stinson Municipal Airport.
- 9.6 Pass 99th St. intersection.
- 10.3 At stop sign T intersection, very carefully turn left, crossing six lanes of traffic, onto SE Military Dr.
- 10.4 Bear right to continue onto Mission Rd.
- 10.9 At stop sign turn left onto Napier.
- 11.0 Turn right onto San José. You may have to cycle around some ongoing construction in front of Mission San José to get to the main entrance.
- 11.1 Turn right onto E. Pyron at the side entrance to Mission San José.
- 11.5 Turn left onto Padre.
- 12.2 Turn right briefly onto E. White St.
- 12.3 Turn left onto Mission Pkwy.
- 13.5 Turn right onto Mission Rd.
- 14.3 Finish at entrance to Mission Concepción.

31

La Bahia Challenge

Goliad—Weesatche—Weser—Ander—Goliad

Travelers through south Texas know Goliad as a main crossroad on the way to Gulf Coast beaches, the Rio Grande Valley, and Mexico. Goliad has been a main Texas crossroad for hundreds of years. The town is filled with significant historic sites and friendly people and merits a special visit.

Although the back roads of Goliad County are known to cyclists from Corpus Christi, they remain relatively undiscovered by other riders. This may change through the efforts of people like Faye Irby, who helps promote a nice bike tour each October. Faye can tell you about other good roads to ride nearby, including the route of the Missions Tour de Goliad. You'll find her at her store, Faye's Naturals, on the town square where these routes begin.

This is the area of Spain's earliest Texas settlements. The routes set out here travel north of town, through countryside where the Spanish first introduced cattle ranching to North America. Cattle ranching, farming, and hunting remain the principal activities in the small communities these roads pass through.

Goliad is among the oldest municipalities in the state. The first American colonies in Texas were connected to this important south Texas settlement by the famous La Bahia Road, and Goliad became a principal link between these colonies and Mexico. The events memorialized by the parks, monuments, and historic sites of Goliad tell much of the story of Texas prior to its statehood.

A Spanish mission called Espiritu Santo and a Spanish military fort known as Presidio La Bahia were the first outposts established in Goliad some three hundred years ago. The mission is preserved today as a unique state park. The fort, one of the most fought-over in Texas history, is a National Historic Landmark. Presidio La Bahia was involved in six separate independence wars and is the focal point of the area's long and colorful military history. Presidio La Bahia is also the site of one of the pivotal events in the fight for Texas's independence from Mexico.

The fort and the mission are not passed on this bike route, but they can be found just a mile or two south of the town square starting point on US 183. Also near the fort and mission on US 183 is the La Bahia Restaurant, a favorite place to eat before or after a ride.

The Basics

Start: At the Goliad County courthouse. There is parking around the town square. Mileage is marked from Commercial St. Goliad is about 150 miles southwest of Houston on US 59 and 75 miles north of Corpus Christi.

Mileage: Options of 51.0 miles, 34.7 miles, or 27.4 miles.

Terrain: Mostly flat, some gently rolling ranch land.

Roads: Mostly quiet country roads. US 183 (used for 1.3 miles) has higher-speed traffic but a wide shoulder.

Food: Several options in Goliad; convenience store and café in Weesatche; station in Weser may be open.

Miles & Directions

- 0.0 Begin at the town square around the Goliad County courthouse. Exit the square on Commercial St. and turn immediately left onto Franklin St.
- 0.3 Turn right onto San Patricio at the stop sign and proceed carefully across Pearl St. (US 59).
- 1.2 Turn left on Ward St.

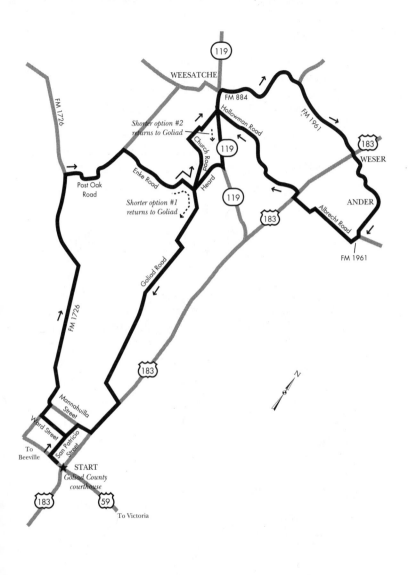

119

WEESATCHE

FM 884

FM 1726

Shorter option #2
returns to Goliad

Hollowman Road

FM 1961

119

183

WESER

Church Road

Post Oak
Road

Enke Road

Heard

119

ANDER

Shorter option #1
returns to Goliad

183

Albrecht Road

FM 1726

Goliad Road

FM 1961

183

Mannahuilla
Street

Ward Street

To
Beeville

San Patricio Street

START
Goliad County
courthouse

183

59

To Victoria

N

- 2.3 At the stop sign, turn right onto FM 1726 (unmarked).
- 10.5 Turn right onto Post Oak Rd.
- 13.0 Turn right onto Enke Rd.
- 15.9 Turn hard left onto Church Rd.

For a shorter option totaling 27.4 miles, continue past the Church Rd. intersection straight onto Goliad Rd. in 0.1 mile. Follow the directions for the full tour from mile 39.6 to return to Goliad.

- 19.4 Turn left onto Texas 119.
- 19.7 Pass convenience stores in Weesatche.

For a shorter option totaling 34.7 miles, turn around and head south on Texas 119. After 2.2 miles turn right onto Heard. Follow the directions for the full tour from mile 38.2 to return to Goliad.

- 19.8 Turn right (east) onto FM 884.
- 23.0 Turn right (east) onto FM 1961.
- 26.1 Cross US 183 at the community of Weser. Store at the Bade Service Station may be open.
- 29.2 After passing through the community of Ander, turn right onto Albrecht Rd.
- 32.1 Turn right onto US 183.
- 32.3 Carefully turn left across traffic onto Hollowman Rd.
- 36.5 Turn left onto Texas 119.
- 38.2 Turn right onto Heard.
- 39.6 Turn left onto the Goliad Rd., where Enke Rd. and Heard converge to become Goliad Rd.
- 47.4 At stop sign, turn right onto US 183.
- 48.7 Turn right onto Mannahuilla.
- 49.3 Turn left onto San Patricio.
- 50.6 Cross Pearl (US 59).
- 50.7 Turn left onto Franklin St.
- 51.0 Turn left onto Commercial St. to finish at the town square.

32

Laguna Atascosa Challenge

Port Isabel—Laguna Vista—Laguna Atascosa
National Wildlife Refuge—Laguna Vista—Port Isabel

There was a time when most of the lower Rio Grande Valley looked like the Laguna Atascosa National Wildlife Refuge. Grassland, wetland, and brushland once covered this part of south Texas inland from the shores of Laguna Madre, the long, narrow bay between the mainland and Padre Island.

Over time, grasslands were overgrazed by cattle, wetlands were bulldozed into fields for sugarcane and cotton, and brushlands were cleared for development. Native vegetation remains in only small areas.

A ride north from the historic lighthouse in Port Isabel passes through cultivated fields and grazing pastures on the way to a magnificent wildlife refuge preserved at Laguna Atascosa. This route can be divided into two shorter options. One visits only the flat farmland now characteristic of most of the countryside in the Rio Grande Valley. The other visits only the carefully preserved habitat within the national wildlife refuge. Combining the two on the full tour illustrates the different ways our environment can be influenced.

The lighthouse in Port Isabel provides a prominent point for the start of this tour. From the top of the 150-year-old lighthouse are sweeping views across the bay to South Padre Island and inland over the countryside of this bike route. Before or after your ride, you can discover plenty of history and plenty of good places to eat in Port Isabel.

Regardless of the bike route you choose, plan to spend some time visiting the wildlife refuge. The habitat preserved in the refuge is thick in winter with migratory waterfowl and is home all year to an exotic cast of residents including ocelots, egrets, herons, cranes, and several threatened and endangered species. The refuge visitors center is a good source of information about habitat management and the other wildlife refuges maintained throughout Texas.

The fifteen-mile loop along Bayside Drive in the refuge is popular with cyclists, but the road surface is only semipaved. It is passable on a road bike but more pleasurable on an all-terrain bike. Despite the poor character of the road surface, this unusual one-way passage, especially the portion paralleling the shore of Laguna Madre, is well worth the effort. The road is lined with interpretive markers describing this habitat and its residents.

Special attention to the elements is warranted on any bike ride in the Rio Grande Valley. The sun and wind are always strong, and there is little shade or protection in this open country. Dress properly, drink often, and use adequate sunscreen.

The Basics

Start: At the Port Isabel Lighthouse, on Queen Isabella Dr. at the base of the causeway. Starting at Port Isabel High School shortens the route by 5.4 miles and eliminates some of the busier parts of Texas 100. Port Isabel is about 125 miles south of Corpus Christi and about 25 miles northeast of the Mexican border at Brownsville.
Distance: 52.4 miles. Bypass the wildlife refuge for a tour of 33.0 miles. From the refuge visitors center, a tour of Bayside Dr. in the wildlife refuge is 14.4 miles.
Terrain: Flat.
Roads: Texas 100 is busy but with a wide shoulder, although some cars use the shoulder for parking in town. FM roads are two lanes, light traffic. County roads are narrow, light traffic. Portions of Bayside Dr. are unpaved and better suited to an all-terrain bike.
Food: Several options in Port Isabel. Store in Laguna Vista. Water and restrooms at visitors center in Laguna Atascosa Wildlife Refuge.

Miles & Directions

- 0.0 Leave Port Isabel Lighthouse by turning right (west) onto Texas 100, called Queen Isabella Blvd. here.
- 2.7 Pass Port Isabel High School.

Using Port Isabel High School as an alternative starting point eliminates some traffic and 5.4 miles.

- 3.6 Pass Laguna Vista town sign. Commercial development ends.
- 5.3 Turn right onto FM 510 (west) at the Laguna Vista sign. Two lanes, wide shoulder.
- 6.0 Pass store, shoulder continues. Nice vegetation lines the road for a while. Where land isn't cultivated, the character of the brushland is interesting. Lose shoulder after 3 miles.
- 10.5 At Y intersection, leave FM 510, which bends left, by following sign to wildlife refuge to the right. Road is unmarked, known locally as Buena Vista or the Cameron County Airport Rd. Two lanes, no shoulder.
- 15.1 Continue straight past intersection of Texas 106 to left (unmarked) at the sign directing traffic to the wildlife refuge. Road narrows, no traffic.

For a shorter option totaling 33.0 miles, turn left here and bypass the Laguna Atascosa National Wildlife Refuge. Follow the directions for the full tour from mile 34.5 to return to Port Isabel. Continuing out-and-back only to the refuge visitors center adds 2.7 miles each way from this point.

- 16.2 Pass sign entering Laguna Atascosa National Wildlife Refuge. Cultivation of surrounding land ends.
- 17.7 Turn right onto Bayside Dr. Semipaved park road with some very rough patches. Open sunrise to sunset. The road is narrow, with interpretive signs along the way.

The visitors center is 0.1 mile further on to the left. Begin a ride on

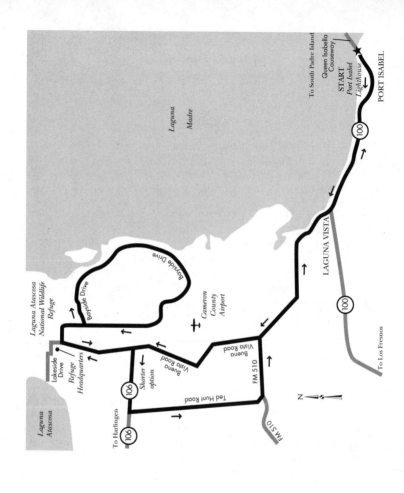

Bayside Dr. from the visitors center for a shorter option totaling 14.4 miles.

Note also that turning left from the visitors center parking lot is Lakeside Dr., a semipaved road for 1.5 miles each way to Osprey Overlook on the shore of Laguna Atascosa.

- 18.6 Road bends left and becomes one way. Rough and unpaved patches of road will continue throughout.
- 19.2 Enter wetlands of Pelican Lake; head toward the shoreline of Laguna Madre.
- 22.5 Nice views from Stover Point. On a clear day you can see the hotels of South Padre Island across the bay.
- 23.9 Past the Redhead Ridge overlook, the road will soon turn back into the refuge away from the bay, where there are fewer interpretive markers.
- 30.9 Traffic becomes two-way.
- 31.9 Turn left at stop sign to leave the refuge.

The refuge visitors center is 0.1 mile to the right.

- 33.4 Pass sign marking entrance to refuge.
- 34.5 Turn right on unmarked Texas 106. Narrow road, no shoulder, through flat fields.
- 36.5 Turn left on Ted Hunt Rd. Also two lanes, no shoulder, through flat fields.
- 38.0 The irrigation canal you're crossing here is called the Rescata de los Cuates.
- 40.9 Turn left at T intersection (unmarked) onto FM 510.
- 42.9 FM 510 bends to the right at the Y intersection with the Cameron County Airport Rd. Bear right to stay on FM 510.
- 46.4 Pass store in Laguna Vista.
- 47.1 Turn left onto Texas 100.
- 49.7 Pass Port Isabel town sign and Port Isabel High School.
- 52.4 Finish across from the Port Isabel Lighthouse. Carefully cross Queen Isabella Blvd. to return to the lighthouse square.

33

South Padre Island Ramble

South Padre Island

The beautiful beaches of South Padre Island are in the Texas tropics, where it's almost always warm. The sun and sea are a draw throughout the year, especially for thousands of "winter Texans" from across the country who flock to the lower Rio Grande valley to escape the cold north.

Padre Island is named for a religious leader of Spanish descent who settled the island at the beginning of the nineteenth century. Today, the Padre's settlement is premium resort property. The southern tip of the island is blanketed by beachfront condominium and hotel development.

Further north on the island are unspoiled beaches and dunes of white sand, which are traveled by horseback riders, dune buggies, and bicycles. There are only three roads running north and south on this thin strip of land, and all three are excellent for cycling. The busier park road in the middle has a wide shoulder, and the two side roads have little traffic.

The ride starts at the island's southern tip at Isla Blanca Park, a prominent county camping facility, and follows Harbor Street on the east side of the island through town and along the shore of the Gulf of Mexico. After rejoining the main park road, there is a nice stretch past the empty beaches and sand dunes further north. The ride returns to town along Laguna Drive on the west side of the island along the Laguna Madre shore, the bay separating the island from the mainland. As befits a beachfront resort, there are all sorts of places to eat and drink back in town after your ride.

Be prepared for intense exposure to the elements during a ride on South Padre Island. The course is perfectly flat, with only a few tall hotels and condominiums on the south side of the island to break the wind or provide shade. The sun is strong, so dress accordingly and use lots of sunscreen. The wind sweeps sand across the roadway, and dunes may encroach onto the road shoulder as you ride further north.

Each February one of the earliest organized rides of the year in Texas for road bikes is the Border Surf and Citrus 100, which combines the roads on South Padre Island with some of the roads on the mainland between Port Isabel and Los Fresnos. To reach the mainland from the island involves a crossing of three miles on the Queen Isabella Causeway. Don't try cycling the causeway without the benefit of traffic control provided by an organized event.

The Basics

Start: At Isla Blanca Park entrance on South Padre Island, just after crossing the Queen Isabella Causeway. There is parking around the park headquarters building. South Padre Island is about 25 miles north of the Mexican border at Brownsville.

Distance: 24.4 miles.

Terrain: Flat.

Roads: Park Rd. 100 has a wide shoulder. Lots of traffic near resort developments. Town roads have a wide lane for public trolleys, but cars park in the lane from time to time.

Food: Several choices on the south half of the island near the resort development.

Miles & Directions

- 0.0 Head north from entrance to Isla Blanca Park.
- 0.4 Traffic island divides the road near the entrance to the Queen Isabella Causeway. Road becomes two lanes going one way with a wide shoulder.
- 0.7 At stop sign, the road becomes Park Rd. 100 as it joins traf-

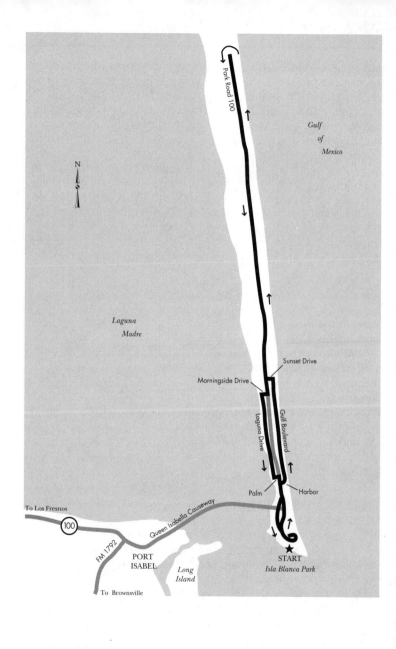

Gulf
of
Mexico

Park Road 100

Laguna
Madre

Sunset Drive

Morningside Drive

Laguna Drive

Gulf Boulevard

Palm

Harbor

To Los Fresnos

100

FM 1792

Queen Isabella Causeway

PORT
ISABEL

Long
Island

To Brownsville

START
Isla Blanca Park

N

fic from the causeway. Continue straight in a northerly direction on Park Rd. 100.

- 1.4 Turn right at first traffic light onto Harbor St.
- 1.5 Turn left at stop sign onto Gulf Blvd. Two lanes, a wide shoulder for trolley shuttle bus, perfectly flat. Ocean views are mostly blocked by hotels here.
- 3.9 When Gulf Blvd. dead-ends, turn left onto Sunset Dr.
- 4.2 Turn right at stop sign back onto Park Rd. 100. Wide shoulder, increased traffic speed.
- 4.8 Road becomes two lanes past convention center to the left, Andy Bowie Park to the right. Wide shoulder continues, but sand dunes begin to encroach on it.
- 5.1 Pass Beach Access Point #3, just before horse stables. Enter isolated, less-developed beach terrain with glimpses of ocean and rolling dunes. Perfectly flat, no trees.
- 9.5 Pass Beach Access Point #4.
- 12.2 Road dead-ends into a large expanse of sand along a great beach. Turn around and head back to town.
- 15.0 Pass Beach Access Point #4. Note signs for private property.
- 19.3 Pass Beach Access Point #3.
- 19.6 Pass convention center to the right, Andy Bowie Park to the left.
- 19.8 Pass South Padre Island town sign.
- 20.5 Turn right at stoplight onto Morningside Dr.
- 20.6 Turn immediately left onto Laguna Dr., a nice, long, flat neighborhood road along the west side of the island. No stops, two lanes, no shoulder, light traffic.
- 22.7 Just before Laguna Dr. dead-ends, turn left onto Palm.
- 22.9 At stop sign, turn right onto Park Rd. 100.
- 23.4 Road becomes a divided highway with two lanes going one way, wide shoulder.
- 23.7 Continue straight at directional for road to Isla Blanca Park.
- 23.8 Continue straight through stop sign. (The turn to cross the causeway is to the right.)
- 24.1 Pass sign for Isla Blanca park.
- 24.4 Finish at Isla Blanca Park entrance.

34

Big Thicket Challenge

*Kountze—Saratoga—Thicket—
Honey Island—Kountze*

This route travels through the southern part of the Big Thicket National Preserve. The National Park Service administers more than 84,000 acres of wooded land in southeast Texas, where an incredible diversity of plant and animal life flourishes. A few miles south of the Big Thicket Information Station—maintained by the park service—is Kountze, the seat of Hardin County and the starting point for this Challenge.

Thick woods and swampy marshes make the terrain here difficult to traverse, so early settlers rarely ventured deep into the area's forests. Relatively unexplored and unique in appearance, the swampy thicket developed an aura of mystery over the years. The Big Thicket is home to almost as many interesting local legends as interesting natural features.

Buddy Moore has lived in Hardin County for the last sixty years or so and has recorded a fair number of these stories and histories. If you're interested in local lore or just a nice visit with a friendly fellow, you should visit Buddy at his Armadillo Mini-Museum in Kountze, just north of the Hardin County courthouse on US 69.

Buddy might tell you how the small community you'll pass through toward the end of your bike ride came to be called Honey Island. According to Buddy, Texans who opposed secession during the Civil War were able to avoid conscription into the Confederate army by hiding in the thicket. They raided wild beehives for honey and left jars of it for sympathetic locals, who took the honey in trade for clothes and food. On your ride you may notice that the area is still an island in the sense that it is accessible only by water. Branches of Cypress Creek surround this tiny plot in all directions.

Buddy might also tell you about the natural light phenomenon along the Bragg Road, which the full tour passes just after the town of Saratoga. Bragg Road follows the path of an abandoned railroad right-of-way, which offers an unusual shorter option to this route. Scientists have come here to study the source of the unexplained points of light in the woods along the roadside. Of course, there are plenty of local explanations for their source. You may find the Bragg Road marked on some area maps as the "Ghost Road."

The ride travels west from Kountze through mostly level terrain near the southern portion of the preserve. A shorter option turns quickly north to Honey Island. The full tour continues on roads that form a rough boundary between areas being developed for their timber and oil resources and areas being preserved in their natural state. The terrain is generally indicative of the southern reaches of the Big Thicket, alternately wooded and swampy, with frequent creek and bayou crossings.

If you don't mind a rougher, unmaintained road surface, Bragg Road provides a quiet shortcut through the woods. Once the path of a railroad line, it is flat and straight, an isolated passage with trees right up to the roadside. The return to Kountze past Honey Island is also along flat roads but with some higher-speed traffic on FM 1293.

The Basics

Start: At the Hardin County courthouse in Kountze. Kountze is 15 miles north of Beaumont on US 287.

Distance: 46.5 miles (40.2 miles using Bragg Rd.). 19.5 miles to Honey Island and back.

Terrain: Fairly flat throughout.

Roads: FM roads are two lanes, no shoulders, light traffic. Bragg Rd. (optional) is unmaintained and rough.

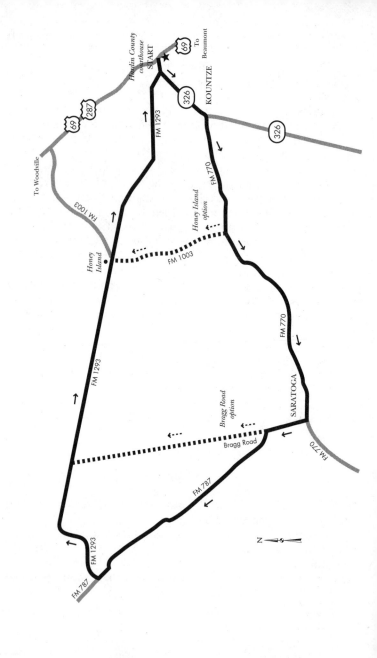

Food: Several stores in Kountze; a store in each of Saratoga, Thicket, and Honey Island.

Miles & Directions

- 0.0 Exit the Hardin County courthouse heading left (south) on Texas 326.
- 0.2 Continue straight past intersection of FM 1293 on the right.
- 2.5 Turn right (south) onto FM 770.
- 7.0 Continue straight past junction of FM 1003 to the right.

For a shorter option totaling 19.5 miles, turn right onto FM 1003, a stretch with a few creek and bayou crossings. After 4.8 miles is the stop sign intersection with FM 1293. The Honey Island General Store is at this corner. Turn right onto FM 1293 and follow directions for the full tour from mile 38.6 to return to Kountze.

- 14.3 Enter Saratoga.
- 15.0 Pass convenience store.
- 15.2 Turn right (west) at the intersection of FM 787.
- 16.8 Past a historical marker about Confederate Civil War General Braxton Bragg, FM 787 bends left at the intersection (unmarked) with Bragg Rd. to the right. The ride from here to the community of Thicket has a flat and swampy character, with nice crossings of Little Pine Island Bayou.

Bragg Road appears unpaved, but underneath a layer of pine needles and dirt is a tightly packed or roughly paved surface. The road is a perfectly flat, one-lane, narrow corridor through the forest, and if you're not in a hurry and don't mind cleaning your bike chain afterwards, you can pick your way along this peaceful path in the heart of the Big Thicket area.

To ride the Bragg Road for a shorter option totaling 40.2 miles, turn right. The only marking is a hand-lettered sign nailed to a tree that says FRESH GOAT HONEY, *but you'll recognize the long, straight corridor ahead as an abandoned railroad right-of-way. Bragg Rd. continues for 7.8 miles until it intersects with FM 1293. Turn right onto FM 1293 and follow directions for the full tour from mile 30.9 to return to Kountze.*

- 25.6 Turn right (east) onto FM 1293 at the Thicket General Store.
- 30.9 Continue straight past the intersection of Bragg Rd. (unmarked) to the right.
- 38.8 Continue straight past the Honey Island General Store.
- 46.3 Turn left (north) onto Texas 326.
- 46.5 Finish at the Hardin County courthouse.

35

Palmetto Cruise

Gonzales—Ottine—Palmetto State Park—Gonzales

The south Texas town of Gonzales was settled in 1825, on a site near the confluence of the Guadalupe and San Marcos rivers. At the time of its settlement Gonzales was remotely located, and the Mexican authorities who administered the area gave the colonists of Gonzales a small brass cannon with which to defend themselves against the Indians.

By 1835 tensions between Mexican authorities and American colonists were high, and Mexican soldiers were sent to Gonzales to reclaim the cannon. The residents of Gonzales refused to give it up, and, daring the soldiers to "come and take it," fired the first shot for Texas independence.

The unique history of Gonzales is preserved today in points of interest along an extensive trail through town that includes historic homesites, buildings, and parks. "Come and Take It Days" celebrations and nearby recreation areas and parks make Gonzales an interesting place to visit.

One of these parks, Palmetto State Park, is the destination for this Cruise, which leaves from Gonzales. The small palmetto palms in the park are one of the many rare species of plant life found in this quiet and lush setting. Because of the diverse vegetation supported in the park, it is also an exceptional birding spot. Texas Parks and Wildlife has catalogued over 240 species of birds that have been sighted within the park or the immediately surrounding area.

This tour is largely an out-and-back ride from Gonzales, with a six-mile loop at the end to take advantage of the beautiful, tree-shaded park road. There is traffic in Gonzales and on the roads leaving town, but as you approach the park, the traffic gradually thins and vegetation begins to fill the open terrain. The prettiest portion of the ride, from park headquarters to a nice scenic overlook, presents a gradual and steady climb for more than a mile. Otherwise, you'll be travelling over rolling terrain.

On your return, you can add six miles to your ride along a quiet road through nice farmlands by traveling out and back on FM 2091 south to Lake Wood. There is a recreational area maintained by the local water authority at this small lake on the Guadalupe River. You can also fashion longer rides along the roads east of Gonzales to the communities of Waelder and Moulton.

The Basics

Start: In Gonzales in front of the Gonzales County courthouse at the corner of St. Joseph's and St. Lawrence streets. There is plenty of parking in the squares next to the courthouse. Gonzales is 60 miles south of Austin and 60 miles north of Goliad on US 183.
Distance: 32.9 miles.
Terrain: Rolling hills.
Roads: St. Lawrence Street and US 183 through town have wide lanes but no shoulders. US 90 and US 183 near the state park have high-speed traffic but extra wide shoulders. FM roads and Park Road 11 are two lanes, no shoulder, light traffic.
Food: Several options in Gonzales; store on Park Road 11; soda machine at park headquarters.

Miles & Directions

- 0.0 Begin in front of Gonzales County courthouse at the corner of St. Lawrence Street (Texas 97) and St. Joseph's Street (Alternate US 183), and head north on St. Joseph's Street through

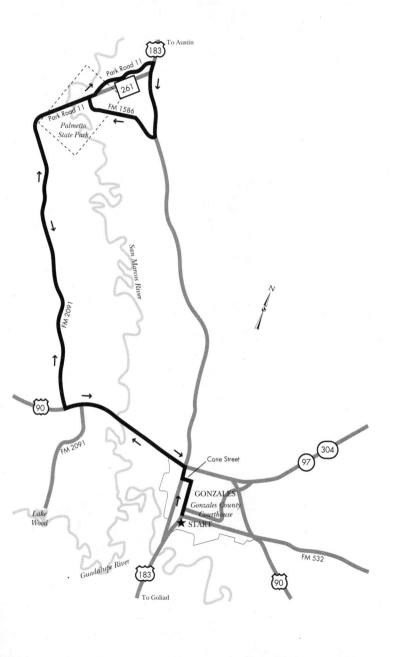

town. Two wide lanes, no shoulder through town. Part of Texas Independence Trail.

- 0.9 Turn left (west) onto Cone Street to avoid busy intersections.
- 1.1 Turn right (north) onto Water Street (US 183), five wide lanes with no shoulder.
- 1.4 Turn left (west) onto US 90 at stoplight intersection. Pick up extra wide shoulder.
- 4.2 Continue straight on US 90 past left turn (south) for FM 2091. This road will dead end at Lake Wood in 3 miles.
- 4.6 Turn right (north) onto FM 2091, following sign to Palmetto State Park. Two lanes, no shoulder, light traffic, rolling hills. Marked as part of the Texas Independence Trail.
- 12.5 Enter Palmetto State Park as FM 2091 combines with Park Road 11. Continue straight past two portions of Park Road 11 that veer right (and dead end at camp grounds).
- 13.0 Cross San Marcos River.
- 13.1 Pass the Ottine town sign.
- 13.4 Continue straight through stop-sign intersection with FM 1586. Park headquarters are on the left.
- 13.5 Pass convenience store.
- 13.6 Bear left to stay on Park Road 11 where County Road 261 veers right. Increasingly forested stretch of road, gradually uphill.
- 15.1 Excellent scenic overlook to the left.
- 15.4 Exit park and turn right (south) onto US 183, which is two lanes with an extra wide shoulder. Be mindful of higher-speed traffic.
- 15.7 Pass intersection with County Road 261.

To avoid 1.5 miles on US 183 and shorten the full tour by 2.1 miles, turn left (west) onto County Road 261, a narrow, quiet lane. After 1.5 miles, turn right (north) onto Park Road 11/FM 2091. After another 0.2 miles, follow the directions from mile 19.5 of the full tour to return to Gonzales.

- 17.3 Turn right (west) onto FM 1586. Two lanes, no shoulder, light traffic. Rolling terrain, open countryside.

- 19.3 Pass Ottine town sign, Warm Springs Rehabilitation Hospital.
- 19.5 Turn left (south) at stop sign onto FM 2091 to return to Gonzales.
- 20.4 Exit Palmetto State Park.
- 28.3 Turn left (east) onto US 90, carefully across traffic, onto extra wide shoulder.
- 31.5 Turn right (south) onto US 183/Water Street at the traffic light.
- 31.8 Turn left (east) very carefully across traffic, onto Cone Street.
- 32.0 Turn right (south) onto Alternate US 183/St. Joseph's Street.
- 32.9 Finish in front of Gonzales County courthouse.

36

Groveton/Davy Crockett National Forest Cruise

Groveton—Centerville—Apple Springs—Groveton

Over one-third of Trinity County is in the Davy Crockett National Forest, the largest of the four national forests in the Piney Woods area of east Texas. There are no major highways in Trinity County, and the communities and towns here are tiny. These features provide a nice setting for cycling through some east Texas woods.

The lumber industry founded and shaped Trinity County, which thrived with the arrival of railroads to east Texas. Groveton, located on the southern end of the Davy Crockett National Forest, is the Trinity County seat and the starting point of this ride.

In the 1870s a sawmill was built in a grove of oak trees here and the spot was named Groveton. A lumber company bought the land and established a town site, which became the county seat after being moved from three previous sites. By 1930, all the timber for miles around had been cut, the sawmill closed, and the once prosperous town went into decline.

The Civilian Conservation Corps was responsible for a road construction and reforestation program during the Depression that restored the area. Today Groveton is best known for its proximity to the recreational areas of Lake Livingston and for the success of its high school football teams.

A bike ride along these roads through the national forest is particularly pleasant in late fall, as there is some nice autumn foliage.

The route heads north and east from Groveton on Texas 94, the road to Lufkin. About halfway to Lufkin, at the community of Apple Springs, the route loops back to Groveton, staying in the national forest for its entire length. A ride on this route is a nice roll through the woods, featuring hilly terrain and crossing small creeks and bayous along the way.

The Basics

Start: Behind the Trinity County courthouse in Groveton. There is parking around the courthouse. Groveton is 120 miles north of Houston and 120 miles east of Waco.
Distance: 37.4 miles.
Terrain: Rolling hills through the forest.
Roads: Some traffic on Texas 94, especially close to Groveton. US 287 (used for 1.4 miles) has high-speed traffic and a wide shoulder until it enters Groveton. Other roads have two lanes, no shoulder, light traffic. Roads are generally a little narrower here.
Food: Stores in Groveton and along Texas 94 at Centerville and Apple Springs.

Miles & Directions

- 0.0 Exit east on Texas 94 behind the Trinity County courthouse, where Texas 94 splits east and west. The street is also called N. Main St. here.
- 2.9 Pass junction of FM 3317 to the right, toward low, long hills with some traffic.
- 6.5 Cross Piney Creek into more thickly forested terrain.
- 8.4 Convenience store here and at mile 8.9, near the Centerville community.
- 9.5 Pass turnoff to FM 358 to the left.
- 14.8 Pass ranger station on the left.
- 15.9 There are two FM road junctions in Apple Springs, where FM 2501 and FM 357 merge. Go past the first turn to the left

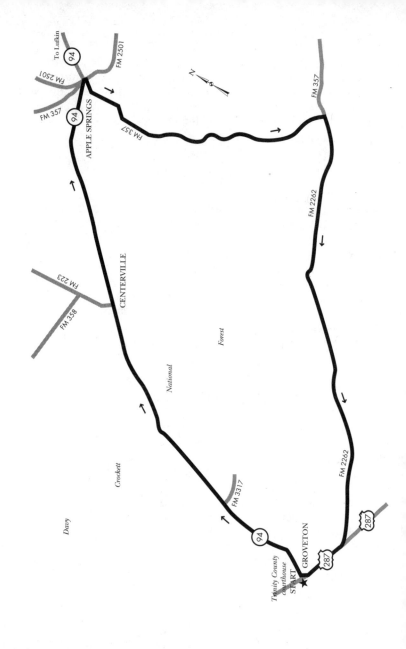

(north) and take the second turn to the right (south) on FM 2501/FM 357, then stay on FM 357 as FM 2501 diverges to the left. There are convenience stores in Apple Springs only. Roads are two lanes, no shoulder, light traffic. There are small family and community cemeteries at several points along the return to Groveton.

- 23.7 At stop sign T intersection, turn right (west) onto FM 2262.
- 33.1 Three crossings of Piney Creek, then through some pastureland among the woods.
- 35.9 Turn right (north) onto US 287 at stop sign T intersection, being mindful of increased traffic. Adequate shoulder.
- 37.0 After entering Groveton, shoulder disappears as US 287 becomes two lanes and is named E. First St. into town.
- 37.3 Turn right at the intersection of Texas 94 and US 287 at the courthouse.
- 37.4 Finish behind courthouse.

Two Coldspring Rambles

Coldspring—Sam Houston National Forest—
Shepherd—Camilla—Coldspring

The U.S. Forest Service administers four national forests in the Piney Woods area of east Texas. The Sam Houston National Forest totals more than 161,000 acres and covers most of San Jacinto County. The town of Coldspring, near the south shore of Lake Livingston, is the seat of this thickly wooded county and the starting point for these bike rides.

Two Rambles, traveling in opposite directions, are set out here for you to explore the eastern part of the Sam Houston National Forest. Combining the two routes totals almost fifty miles of cycling through this popular recreation destination located about an hour's drive north of Houston.

Wilderness areas are preserved throughout sections of the national forests for recreational use. You'll pass two of these areas on the first option, which loops south through Shepherd. Double Lake Recreation Area has swimming, fishing, and camping facilities. Big Creek Scenic Area is all hiking trails, several of which intersect the roads you'll be cycling.

The towns in San Jacinto County are quite small, and much of the property here is used for resort and weekend homes, particularly along the shores of Lake Livingston. The second option takes you north past some of the prettier of these areas, near Wolf Creek and Stephen Creek.

Both routes start in front of the San Jacinto County courthouse, on a quaint town square whose nicely kept and restored buildings house some shops, offices, and places to eat. There are motels and private campgrounds throughout Coldspring for visitors to the forest.

The Basics

Start: At the San Jacinto County courthouse in Coldspring. There is public parking around the courthouse. Coldspring is about 60 miles north of Houston.

Distance: Option one (south toward Shepherd) is 30.7 miles or 24.3 miles. Option two (north toward Wolf Creek) is 18.2 miles.

Terrain: Mostly rolling, fairly gentle terrain.

Roads: Traffic in Coldspring and Shepherd can be heavy. Traffic also may be heavy at times on FM 2025 and Texas 150. Roads are narrow.

Food: Several options in Coldspring; store in Shepherd; stores at Indian Creek Marina and in Evergreen may be open.

Miles & Directions
Option One (south toward Shepherd)

- 0.0 From the intersection with FM 1514 on the town square corner, turn left onto Texas 150, which is Church St. here.
- 0.2 Bear left to stay on Texas 150 at intersection with Texas 156. Texas 150 is two lanes, no shoulder, with traffic through town.
- 1.9 Turn left (south) onto FM 2025, traffic through town continues. Two lanes, no shoulder.
- 2.3 Pass entrance to Double Lake, a recreation area in the Sam Houston National Forest. Excellent colors in the fall.
- 7.5 Turn left (east) at the intersection of FM 2666 toward Big Creek Scenic Area and town of Shepherd; much less traffic but still two lanes, no shoulder.
- 10.0 Pass dirt road entrance to Big Creek Scenic Area.

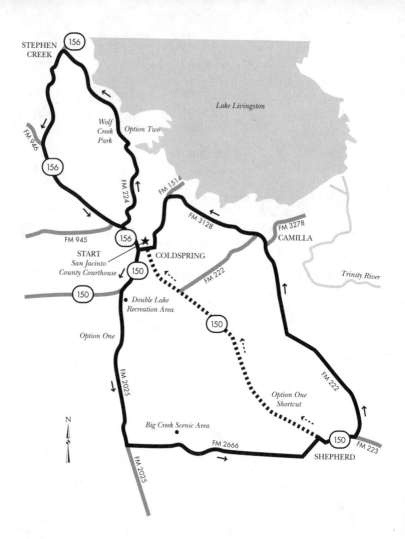

- 14.8 At stop sign intersection, turn right (east) on Texas 150 into Shepherd. No shoulder, high-speed traffic.

For a shorter option totaling 24.3 miles, turn left on Texas 150 and return to the town square in Coldspring.

- 16.1 Turn left (north) onto FM 222 toward Camilla. There is a convenience store near this corner. Road is also called Spring Ave.
- 24.2 Pass Camilla town sign and continue through more open, less-forested country.
- 24.5 Pass intersection of FM 3278 on the right.
- 24.8 Turn right onto FM 3128.
- 28.4 Turn left onto FM 1514.
- 30.7 Finish at town square.

Option Two (north toward Wolf Creek)

- 0.0 From the intersection with FM 1514 on the town square corner, turn left onto Texas 150, which is Church St. here.
- 0.2 Turn right onto Texas 156, marked as the Texas Forest Trail. Adequate shoulder.
- 1.3 Turn right (north) onto FM 224 toward Wolf Creek Park. This nice road is twisted and hilly, with some distant views of Lake Livingston.
- 4.3 Pass Indian Creek Marina.
- 5.8 After passing golf course, some lakeshore views appear.
- 6.1 Pass entrance to Wolf Creek Park.
- 8.0 Pass Stephen Creek town sign.
- 9.1 Turn left (south) at stop sign T intersection with Texas 156; adequate shoulder all the way back to Coldspring.
- 12.8 Continue straight on Texas 156 past the intersection of FM 946.
- 16.6 Pass intersection of FM 945 to the right.
- 18.0 Turn left onto Texas 150.
- 18.2 Finish at the town square.

38

Grimes County Cruise

Anderson—Carlos—Roan's Prairie—Anderson

A ride through the countryside of Grimes County passes along roadways that brought some of the first explorers and settlers to Texas. French and Spanish colonists staked claims to the area, and two of Stephen F. Austin's original colonists acquired one of the earliest grants from Mexico here. The county seat of Anderson was a prominent crossroad for these early claimants of Texas territory.

When France attempted to expand its empire in the Americas during the seventeenth century, it briefly became one of the "six flags" to assert national sovereignty over Texas. The explorer LaSalle landed on the Texas Gulf Coast to stake a French claim and began moving inland, but he died soon after near Navasota, some ten miles to the southwest of the start of this route.

A French presence continued here during the eighteenth century. Slaves and other goods were smuggled into Louisiana over roads that came to be known as the Contraband Trail. The Spanish responded with increased expeditions to the area along the nearby La Bahia Road and El Camino Real, the main thoroughfares of early Texas.

Anderson became the county seat shortly after Texas statehood, and Grimes County prospered from the cotton it produced. The restored Fanthorp Inn, now a state park, was built in 1834 and retains for Anderson some of the look and feel of that time. The inn and the town were prominent as an important stop on early stagecoach routes, and weekend stagecoach rides are still offered periodically from the inn.

Anderson today has only three hundred residents, making it one of the smaller county seats in Texas. It's a pleasant place to visit and is near several other points of interest. To the southwest is Navasota, a much larger town with an interesting history, and a few miles further on is the historic Washington-on-the-Brazos State Park, a favorite spot on the **Washington-on-the-Brazos Challenge**. College Station, home of Texas A & M University, is a half-hour drive to the northwest; an entrance to the Sam Houston National Forest is a few miles to the east.

The Grimes County courthouse sits on a small hill in the center of town and is Anderson's dominant feature. Leaving the courthouse and heading west along farm roads, you'll cross a few small creeks and have a partly shaded ride along roads with some rough surfaces. Be prepared for high-speed traffic on the state highways north of Anderson. The FM roads to the east on the final leg pass through open pastureland, with some more rough surfaces closer to town.

The Basics

Start: At the Grimes County courthouse in Anderson. Anderson is 10 miles northeast of Navasota and 30 miles east of College Station.
Distance: 35.2 miles or 22.0 miles.
Terrain: Some rolling hills, mostly gentle.
Roads: Surfaces on the FM roads in this area are generally rough, especially along FM 3090 and FM 149 to the east. Traffic on Texas 30 can be heavy, and it has little or no shoulder.
Food: Stores in Anderson, Carlos, and Roan's Prairie.

Miles & Directions

- 0.0 Leave the Grimes County courthouse, heading north on Loop 429 toward FM 149.
- 0.2 Turn left (south) onto FM 149 and immediately left again onto Texas 90.

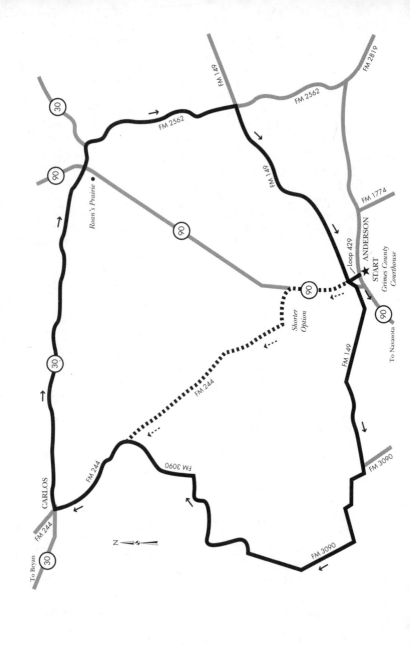

- 0.3 Turn right (west) to continue on FM 149.
- 4.7 At junction of FM 3090, continue straight (north) on FM 3090, along a road with patches of rough surface.
- 14.6 Pass the junction of FM 244 to the right by bearing left onto FM 244 toward Carlos. Two lanes, no shoulder, light traffic, ongoing road-improvement construction.

For a shorter option totaling 22.0 miles, bear right onto FM 244. After 5.7 miles turn right (south) onto Texas 90. Continue on Texas 90 for another 1.5 miles (there's a nice view of the courthouse from a small rise as you enter Anderson) to the intersection of FM 149. Turn left (east) on FM 149 and immediately right onto Loop 429 to finish at the courthouse.

- 17.1 Reach community of Carlos and at stop sign T intersection turn right (east) onto Texas 30. There is a convenience store at this corner. Texas 30 is hilly, challenging, with higher-speed traffic, and no shoulder. Some long, straight-ahead views.
- 25.2 Continue straight past intersection with Texas 90 at stop sign in Roan's Prairie. There is a store here.
- 25.8 Turn right (south) onto FM 2562 through some nice pastureland and meadowland.
- 29.8 Turn right (west) onto FM 149. Open pastureland predominant at first but some rolling hills closer to Anderson. Road surface may be rough.
- 35.0 Turn left on Loop 429 toward courthouse.
- 35.2 Finish at the Grimes County courthouse.

39

Washington-On-the-Brazos Challenge

Chappell Hill—Washington-on-the-Brazos State Park—Chappell Hill

For idyllic pastureland, spectacular spring wildflowers, and historic interest, a ride along the roads between the village of Chappell Hill and the Washington-on-the-Brazos State Park is hard to beat. This rural area can be reached from metropolitan Houston in less than an hour's drive.

Close by are other interesting towns to visit, with or without your bicycle. Brenham, site of the **Blue Bell Ramble**, is a few miles farther west. Navasota, near the start of the **Grimes County Cruise**, is just northeast of the park.

Chappell Hill is a convenient and fun place to begin a tour of this area, and it allows a longer ride along these lovely roads. Many of the older buildings lining the main street in Chappell Hill have been restored and house nice shops and places to eat. There is public parking on the streets in this renovated district and at the museum located off the main road.

Directions for shorter loops over these same roads, starting from the beautiful state historical park on the Brazos River, are included. The park preserves the sites of the signing of the Texas Declaration of Independence, drafting of the republic's constitution, home of the republic's last president, and location of the first capital of the state. The park is just a few miles from Navasota and is worth a visit regardless of where you choose to start your ride. Note that the park closes at sunset and does not have facilities for camping, but it is an excellent site for picnicking and day trips.

Permanent settlement here dates from the arrival of Stephen F. Austin's original colonists in the 1820s. The community of Washington began as a ferry crossing of the river the Spanish first called *Los Brazos del Dios*, "the arms of God," for the effect it had on the fertile countryside. This is still rich farmland for the residents of this part of Washington County, including the interesting Peaceable Kingdom community a few miles north of the park. Innovative land management and conservation techniques are on display through tours at the Peaceable Kingdom School.

These roads, which once carried Spanish traders, Mexican armies, and Texas colonists, now carry carloads of sightseers when wildflowers are in bloom. The sights are spectacular in the spring, so be mindful of increased traffic during your rides here in springtime.

The Basics

Start: At the intersection of FM 2447 and FM 1155 in Chappell Hill. There is parking along Main St. (FM 1155) and on side streets in town. The shorter options begin at the entrance to Washington-on-the-Brazos State Park, which has public parking but which closes at sunset. Chappell Hill is 50 miles west of Houston on US 290.

Length: 41.9 miles from Chappell Hill. 21.0 miles or 13.2 miles from Washington-on-the-Brazos State Park.

Terrain: Gently rolling hills.

Roads: FM roads are two lanes, no shoulders, light traffic except during spring wildflower season. Texas 105 has higher-speed traffic, wide shoulder.

Food: Lots of choices in Chappell Hill; water and restrooms at the park; Stolz's Grocery may be open in Washington.

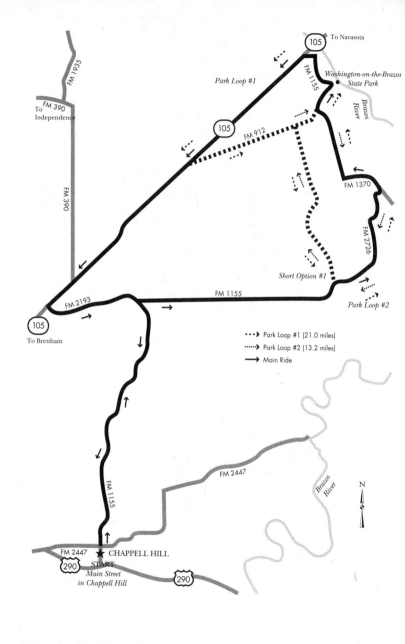

FM 1935

FM 390
To
Independence

FM 390

FM 2193

105
To Brenham

105
To Navasota

Park Loop #1

FM 1155

Washington-on-the-Brazos State Park

Brazos River

105   FM 912

FM 1370

FM 2726

Short Option #1

Park Loop #2

FM 1155

- - -► Park Loop #1 (21.0 miles)
······► Park Loop #2 (13.2 miles)
——► Main Ride

FM 2447

Brazos River

N

FM 1155

FM 2447   ★ CHAPPELL HILL
290   START
Main Street in Chappell Hill

290

Miles & Directions

- **0.0** Head north on FM 1155 out of Chappell Hill from the stop sign intersection of FM 2447 and FM 1155.
- **7.3** Bear right and stay on FM 1155 at intersection with FM 2193.
- **12.9** Bear right onto FM 2726.

You can shorten your ride by 1.2 miles by continuing on FM 1155 past this intersection. After 5.4 miles, you'll rejoin the full tour at mile 19.5.

- **16.2** Bear left onto FM 1370.
- **19.5** Turn right onto FM 1155.
- **20.1** Pass entrance to Washington-on-the-Brazos State Park. It's 0.4 mile to park headquarters on the park road.
- **20.3** Continue on FM 1155 as it bears hard left past the Stolz Grocery Store and the Washington post office.
- **21.7** Traffic circle marks intersection with Texas 105. Turn left (west) onto Texas 105.
- **26.2** Pass FM 912.
- **31.8** Carefully turn left across traffic onto FM 2193 past convenience store.
- **34.6** Turn right onto FM 1155.
- **41.9** Finish at intersection of FM 1155 and FM 2447 in Chappell Hill.

Two Shorter Loops Starting at Washington-on-the-Brazos State Park

- **0.0** Exit park to the left.
- **0.6** Turn left onto FM 1370.
- **3.9** Turn right onto FM 2726.
- **7.2** Turn right onto FM 1155.
- **11.8** Turn left onto FM 912.

For a ride of 13.2 miles, bear right at the intersection with FM 912 and stay on FM 1155 to return to the park.

- 14.9 Turn right onto Texas 105, mindful of higher speed traffic.
- 19.4 Turn right at the traffic circle onto FM 1155.
- 21.0 Finish at park entrance.

40

Blue Bell Ramble

Brenham—Prairie Hill—Independence—
Prairie Hill—Brenham

This route starts on the east side of town at "the little creamery in Brenham," as the Blue Bell Creameries refers to itself. This facility has been making delicious ice cream here since 1907. A favorite piece of their advertising attributes the great taste of Blue Bell Ice Cream to local ingredients. The milk is of such high quality, they say, because the cows think Brenham is heaven.

You'll see plenty of these happy cows as you ride through their pastureland on the way to historic Independence, now a tiny but attractive spot north of Brenham. Independence was founded as Coles Settlement on a grant of land obtained from Mexico, just after it became independent of Spain. The name of Independence was taken a few years later as a part of the Republic of Texas, just after it became independent of Mexico.

Tiny Independence lost a heated fight to Brenham to become county seat of Washington County. Instead it became home to many famous figures from Texas's early days. Several interesting historic churches, home sites, and cemeteries remain, and the nearby Antique Rose Emporium adds special beauty to an already beautiful area.

FM 390 through Independence is specially designated as a state scenic road, and the spring wildflower displays there are stunning. This bike route travels only a short way on FM 390, which was originally part of the La Bahia Road connecting early Texas settlements here to Goliad and south Texas and from there to the interior of Mexico. If you decide on a longer side trip along this roadway in the springtime, be aware that sightseers in passing vehicles may be more intent on watching for wildflowers than for cyclists.

The return from Independence to Brenham passes through picturesque pastureland filled with dairy cows. There is a nice approach to the Lutheran church at Prairie Hill and some water crossings back to town along the Old Independence Road. At the end of this road is the Washington County Fairgrounds, which has lots of public parking and provides an alternate location to start and finish your ride. Although the Blue Bell facility is open to the public for tours on weekdays, it is a private business, so be sure to ask about parking there if that's where you're starting your ride.

Back in Brenham there are interesting places to visit in town, especially around the town square. If the Blue Bell Creamery and gift shop is closed, you'll still find lots of fresh ice cream available all over town. There's nothing like a few scoops of Blue Bell Pecan Pralines and Cream after a bike ride from Brenham.

The Basics

Start: At the Blue Bell Creameries in Brenham (exit US 290 at FM 577). The Blue Bell parking lot is part of a private business and busy with tours during the week, so ask about parking there. There is public parking around the Washington County Fairgrounds (at mile 1.4 of the tour). Brenham is 60 miles east of Houston on US 290.
Length: 29.6 miles from the Blue Bell Creamery; 26.8 miles from the Washington County Fairgrounds.
Terrain: Gently rolling pastureland.
Roads: FM roads are two lanes, no shoulder. FM 50 may have heavy traffic, and during the spring wildflower season, all area roads have traffic. The county roads are isolated, and one small stretch of the Old Independence Rd. is poorly surfaced.
Food: Several options in Brenham; one store in Independence.

Miles & Directions

- 0.0 Exit Blue Bell Creameries and turn right (north) on FM

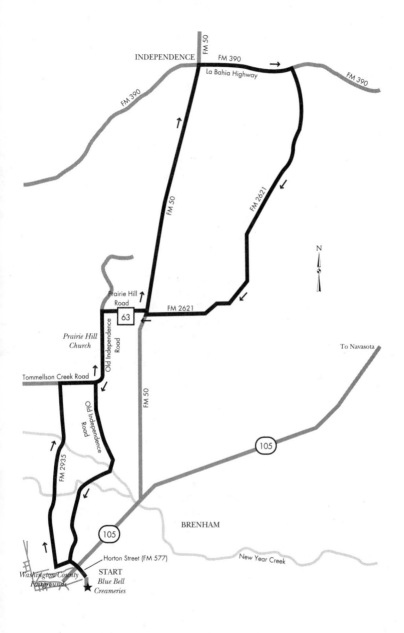

577/Horton St., which has a shoulder and high-speed traffic.

- 0.3 Cross railroad tracks.
- 1.2 Continue straight through stoplight intersection of Texas 105.
- 1.4 Pass Washington County Fairgrounds and intersection of Old Independence Rd. to the right. (Your ride will be 26.8 miles if you start it from this point.)
- 1.7 Turn right (north) onto FM 2935.
- 5.4 At stop sign T intersection with Tommellson Creek Rd., turn right.
- 6.1 Road bends to the left past the unmarked intersection with Old Independence Rd. to the right. Tommellson Creek Rd. has merged with Old Independence Rd. here and is also marked as Washington County Rd. 60.
- 7.5 After passing Prairie Vale Ranch and Prairie Hill Cemetery, turn right onto Prairie Hill Rd./Washington County Rd. 63. Prairie Hill Lutheran Church is to the left.
- 8.3 Turn left (north) onto FM 50 across from Hackberry Hill Farm, being attentive to increased traffic.
- 12.9 Pass Independence town sign.
- 13.3 Turn right (east) on the La Bahia Hwy. (scenic FM 390) in Independence, past historical sites and markers. Pass convenience store to the right (mile 13.5).
- 15.2 Turn right (south) onto FM 2621, through pastureland and past dairy cows.
- 21.9 Turn right at T intersection with FM 50 and then immediately left onto Prairie Hill Rd., with a nice approach to the church.
- 22.8 Turn left onto Old Independence Rd.
- 24.2 Bear left to stay on Old Independence Rd. at the unmarked intersection with Tommellson Creek Rd.
- 25.8 Bear right at Y intersection, staying on Old Independence Rd. Cross creek and unpaved section about 0.2 mile long.
- 28.1 Pass Washington County Fairgrounds on right.
- 28.2 Turn left onto FM 577/Horton St.
- 29.6 Finish at the Blue Bell Creameries.

41

Austin's Colony Cruise

Fayetteville—Lone Oak—Frelsburg—New Ulm—
Industry—Willow Springs—Fayetteville

When Moses Austin and his son, Stephen F. Austin, secured the right to settle American immigrants in Texas, one of the conditions imposed by the new Mexican government was that at least three hundred families must settle in the lands of their grant between the Brazos and Colorado rivers. Many of the settlements staked out by what came to be know as the "original three hundred" of Austin's families grew into the present-day communities found within the borders of what was then known as Austin's Colony.

There were other requirements imposed on these original settlers in order to secure title to these lands. To coordinate the supervision, settlement, surveying, and other tasks required for these settlements to take root, Austin established a capital for his colony on the Brazos River at San Felipe, in the southeast of present-day Austin County. Settlements, stagecoach routes, and other services spread out from here across the area of the colony, which extends through parts of several counties today.

This bike route passes through a handful of the settlements of the original three hundred that are immediately west of Austin's first colonial capital. Although founded by the Anglo families that arrived with Austin, the towns that grew up around these settlements were populated by German and Czech immigrants who began arriving soon after Austin's families. As a result, the area retains a strong German heritage, which is reflected in town names, architecture, and residents.

The tour begins in Fayetteville, established by three of Austin's original three hundred families. In the town square of this village is a marker denoting Fayetteville as a stagecoach stop on the San Felipe Trail, which connected Austin's first capital with Goliad and Presidio La Bahia to the south.

This ride passes through the farmland and ranch land of a handful of small communities, and the route briefly leaves FM roads for country lanes past Lone Oak for an even quieter tour of this terrain. The road passes through Frelsburg and New Ulm, two more communities staked out by Austin's colonists and subsequently settled by German immigrants. Further on is Industry, dating from 1830 and generally regarded as the first of the German communities in Texas.

On the way back to Fayetteville, it's possible to extend your ride through the heart of Austin's Colony by combining it with the **Round Top Ramble** to the north. The communities of Shelby, Winedale, Round Top, and Warrenton featured on that ride have similar origins, having also been founded by members of Austin's "original three hundred" and subsequently populated by German immigrants.

The Basics

Start: Town square off Main St. in Fayetteville.
Distance: 35.4 miles.
Terrain: Gently rolling terrain through pastureland.
Roads: Lightly traveled roads; some traffic around Industry on FM 109 and Texas 159.
Food: Several choices in Fayetteville and Industry. A store in each of Lone Oak, Frelsburg, New Ulm, and Willow Springs.

Miles & Directions

- 0.0 Starting in the town square, turn left onto Main St. at the corner of Live Oak St.

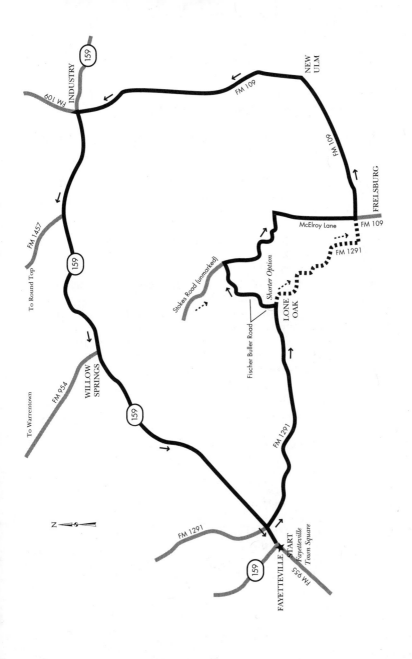

- 0.1 Turn right onto FM 1291.
- 0.2 Cross railroad tracks.
- 3.2 Enter Colorado County. Road is two lanes, light traffic, some rolling hills, and wooded terrain.
- 5.8 Pass Lone Oak town sign.
- 6.0 Turn left onto Fischer Buller Rd., just before an old store. This road is a narrower country lane.

To shorten this route by 2.9 miles, continue straight here. After 3.9 miles, come to FM 109 intersection and follow directions for the full tour from mile 12.8.

- 7.1 Cross railroad tracks. The road narrows and has some rough surfaces.
- 7.2 Bear right at Y intersection.
- 8.1 At the unmarked stop sign intersection, turn right onto a wider road. This is Stokes Rd.
- 9.3 Bear right following the paved road onto McElroy La.
- 10.4 Cross railroad tracks.
- 12.8 Pass store at stop sign intersection with FM 109 and FM 1291 in the town of Frelsburg. Turn left (north) on FM 109.
- 15.6 Enter Austin County.
- 16.2 Pass New Ulm town sign.
- 16.6 Cross railroad tracks.
- 16.7 Pass general store and intersection of FM 1094, continuing straight on FM 109. Two lanes, rolling terrain, some traffic.
- 22.3 Pass Industry town sign.
- 22.6 Turn left (west) at stop sign intersection with Texas 159. There is a store here. Two lanes, open country, shoulder only for 0.5 mile.
- 25.1 Pass FM 1457 junction. Round Top is 13 miles north.

For a longer option totaling 57.2 miles along the roads connecting the settlements of Austin's Colony, you can combine the Round Top Ramble by turning right onto FM 1457 and following the directions for the Round Top Ramble in a reverse (counterclockwise) direction. This intersection is the 13.0 mile mark of the Round Top Ramble.

You'll rejoin Austin's Colony Cruise 3.7 miles down the road, at the general store in Willow Springs where FM 954 intersects Texas 159. Turn right and follow the directions for Austin's Colony Cruise from mile 28.9 back to Fayetteville.

- 27.4 Enter Fayette County, through open country and big fields.
- 28.8 Pass Willow Springs town sign.
- 28.9 Pass general store at the junction of FM 954.
- 29.9 Pass historical marker describing early settlers and marking site of first Fayette County school.
- 30.9 Cross Cummins Creek.
- 32.2 Pass Rek Hill town sign.
- 34.9 Pass Fayetteville town sign.
- 35.2 Texas 159 becomes Main St. and merges with FM 1291 (Thompson St.). Stay on Main St.
- 35.4 Finish at the town square.

42

Round Top Ramble

*Round Top—Winedale—Shelby—
Willow Springs—Warrenton—Round Top*

The original three hundred families who came to settle Texas with Stephen F. Austin, along with the German communities that grew up around them, were connected by trace roads and mail routes. In 1835 a post office and stagecoach stop was established on the main road from the colony's relocated capital at Washington-on-the-Brazos to Goliad in the south, at the site of a settlement whose most prominent feature was "the building with the round top." Of the many communities founded along these early roads, Round Top maintains perhaps the most distinctive charm and interest.

Homes along the early stage roads doubled as inns, where travelers found a spare room and shared family meals. In the early years of Texas settlement, stage lines were dependent on these homes for passenger accommodations. A bike ride around Round Top passes many restored old homes in quaint settings that serve as inns and bed-and-breakfasts for travelers today. Musicians, tourists, and students of history are drawn to this small community halfway between Austin and Houston on the Texas Independence Trail.

The ride leaves Round Top from Henkel Square, at the intersection of Texas 237 (Washington Street) and FM 1457 (Main Street). There is parking, along with a café, antiques store, and post office around this small square. A short distance from Round Top down a side road is the Winedale community, with a unique historical center maintained by the University of Texas. Among the center's attractions are a museum and institute for the study of the ethnic cultures of central Texas, a collection of restored plantation and farm buildings, and summer Shakespeare workshops.

Past Winedale, the route continues through the crossroad at the Shelby community, settled in 1822 by one of the original colonists to arrive with Stephen F. Austin. The route briefly connects with the route of **Austin's Colony Cruise** near the Willow Springs community before turning north toward Warrenton—another site established by one of Austin's families—and then past bed-and-breakfast accommodations back into Round Top.

You'll want to combine your bike ride from Round Top with a visit to the beautiful grounds and buildings of nearby Festival Hill, about a mile or so north of the route's starting point. Festival Hill is an internationally known classical music teaching and performance center. There are wonderful concerts during the summer and at other times during the year at Festival Hill.

The Basics

Start: At Henkel Square in Round Top, the intersection of Texas 237 and FM 1457. Round Top is about 85 miles west of Houston and 25 miles southwest of Brenham.
Distance: 29.2 miles or 21.0 miles.
Terrain: Gently rolling through wooded pastureland.
Roads: FM roads are lightly traveled; a little more, but not much, traffic on Texas 237.
Food: Options in Round Top; stores in Willow Springs and near Warrenton.

Miles & Directions

- 0.0 Exit town square on FM 1457 heading east. Two lanes, no shoulder.
- 0.4 Pass Round Top town sign into some rolling, nicely wooded pastureland.

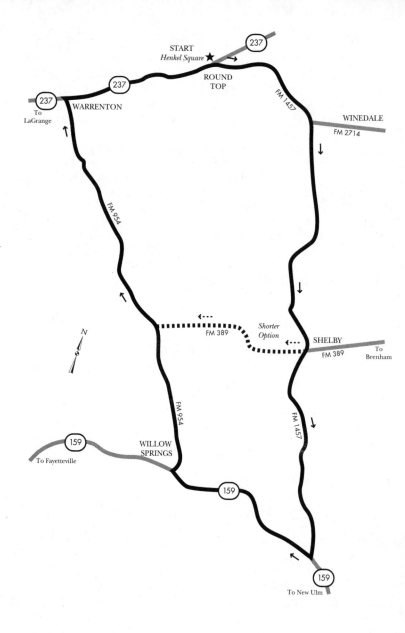

- 2.7 Pass junction FM 2714 north.

Winedale historical center is 1.5 miles to the left on FM 2714, after which the pavement ends. A restored nineteenth-century farmstead is maintained on the grounds, complete with plantation homes, log cabins, barns, and smokehouses.

- 7.0 Enter Austin County, passing through woods, meadows, and gently rolling terrain.
- 8.1 Enter Shelby and continue straight on FM 1457 past the junction of FM 389.

For a shorter option totaling 21.0 miles, turn right onto FM 389 and continue for 3.8 miles to the intersection of FM 954. Turn right and follow the directions for the full tour from mile 20.1 to return to Round Top.

- 9.2 Pass historical marker describing early settlers.
- 13.0 Turn right at stop sign onto Texas 159.

This intersection is also mile 25.1 of Austin's Colony Cruise. The two routes overlap for 3.7 miles. The directions for Austin's Colony Cruise offer suggestions for a longer ride along roads of similar character.

- 16.6 Pass Willow Springs town sign.
- 16.7 Turn right onto FM 954 past the general store.
- 20.1 Pass FM 389. The shorter option rejoins the full tour here.
- 23.7 Pass Cordes Corner store.
- 25.7 Turn right at stop sign intersection onto Texas 237. Two lanes, some traffic, passing trees, meadows, and bed-and-breakfasts.

To the left in Warrenton in 0.4 mile are convenience stores.

- 28.7 Pass Round Top town sign.
- 29.2 Finish at Henkel Square.

West Texas
and the Texas Panhandle

West Texas and the Texas Panhandle

43

Buffalo Gap Cruise

Buffalo Gap—View—Abilene State Park—
Buffalo Gap

The village of Buffalo Gap makes a good starting point for bike rides through the countryside near Abilene. This small town is located just south of Abilene, a principal commercial center on what was once the edge of the west Texas frontier. Abilene was established by cattlemen as a shipping point for livestock, and major cattle trails and railroad lines converged here.

Buffalo Gap was settled at a natural pass in the Callahan Divide, along trails worn by the buffalo that once inhabited the area. It was also a stop on the principal cattle trails for the large herds driven to Abilene from ranges further west. Today Buffalo Gap is the site of pleasant shops and a restored historic village.

This route heads north from Buffalo Gap, away from the hills of the divide and along the path of the old cattle trails toward Abilene. About halfway to Abilene at the community of View, the route turns west and heads back into hillier terrain.

Leaving View, the ride continues on US 277, which has some traffic but either wide shoulders or a climbing lane to accommodate bicycles. There are some nice views on this road, which becomes increasingly hillier as it continues further into the Callahan Divide. This divide is referred to locally as the Callahan Mountains, but it is really a ridge resulting from the erosion of a sandstone and shale plateau.

The route turns east at Coronado's Camp Store, where a historical marker suggests that the famous Spanish explorer may have passed this way during his travels in 1541. The route continues on a hilly course along a quieter road past Lake Abilene and the Abilene State Park. Red clay and sandstone give this part of the ride a distinctive look.

Upon returning to Buffalo Gap, the main street winds through town past some pretty homes in shaded settings. Though the road seems to change its name through town at almost every block, it is easy to follow back to the Old Settlers Reunion Grounds. It's only a short distance off the main road to the Buffalo Gap Historic Village, an interesting collection of restored structures that preserve some of the flavor of the original settlement here.

The Basics

Start: At the Old Settlers Reunion Grounds in Buffalo Gap on FM 89 (marked as the corner of Vine and Williams). There is also parking along the side streets of the nearby Buffalo Gap Historic Village. Buffalo Gap is 13 miles south of Abilene.
Distance: 28.0 miles.
Terrain: Rolling hills with some climbs on US 277 and FM 89. Flat stretches on FM 1235.
Roads: FM roads are two lanes, no shoulder, light traffic. US 277 has high-speed traffic and a wide shoulder, except on hills where the shoulder becomes an extra climbing lane for traffic.
Food: Several choices in Buffalo Gap; convenience store in View; Coronado's Camp Store.

Miles & Directions

- 0.0 Leave the Old Settlers Reunion Grounds heading north on Vine St. There are several street name changes (including West St., Appleton St., and FM 89). Follow this main street through town.
- 0.9 Turn left onto FM 1235 past the country store.

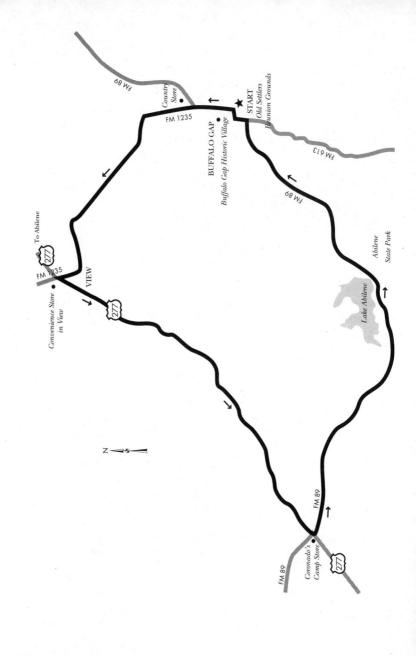

- 5.3 Cross railroad tracks.
- 6.8 At View, carefully turn left (south) across lanes of traffic onto US 277. A convenience store is at this corner. US 277 has higher-speed traffic and rougher pavement at first. This section is very hilly, with some nice views.
- 15.7 Turn left (east) onto FM 89. Coronado's Camp Store is on the right at this intersection. Two lanes, no shoulder, hilly.
- 22.2 Pass access to Lake Abilene on left.
- 23.3 Pass entrance to Abilene State Park on the right.
- 25.9 Pass Buffalo Gap Cemetery.
- 27.2 Cross railroad tracks and enter Buffalo Gap.
- 27.4 Turn left (north) to stay on FM 89 at stop sign intersection with FM 613, which bears right. FM 89, marked as the Texas Forts Trail, winds through town and changes names several times. Stay on the main road.
- 28.0 Finish at the Old Settlers Reunion Grounds.

44

Rails-to-Trails Ramble

Quitaque—Caprock Canyons State Park—Quitaque

Quitaque (pronounced KITTY-quay) is a tiny town in the southeast portion of the Texas Panhandle. It sits along a scenic escarpment that divides the plains through this part of west Texas. Caprock Canyons State Park is north of town, a great place for lovers of the outdoors to visit and explore.

In the spring of 1993, the first segment of the largest rail-to-trail conversion in Texas was opened to the public here. The Caprock Canyons Trailway now extends sixty-four miles through the Texas Panhandle, with Quitaque at the center. As a result, the residents of Quitaque have taken to cycling with a passion.

The Caprock Bicycle Club counts some 5 percent of the town's five hundred residents as active members. Mountain biking along the trailway and the paths in the state park is their principal focus. Ray Stark, one of the club principals, says there is some sort of group ride almost every weekend.

The trailway is a multi-use trail for mountain biking, hiking, and horseback riding along an abandoned railroad right-of-way. It features a 1,000-foot tunnel and passes through several small communities. With its rough, unpaved surface, the trailway is not recommended for road bikes. The area has plenty of paved roads to cycle, though, and is worth a visit with either a mountain bike or a road bike.

The Rails-to-Trails Conservancy is a terrific resource for information about the establishment and use of "Rail Trails." The conservancy's stated mission is "to enhance America's communities and countrysides by converting thousands of miles of abandoned rail corridors, and connecting open space, into a nationwide network of public trails."

The conversion of abandoned railroad rights-of-way to recreational pathways is relatively new in Texas. The few currently established Texas trails are unpaved and, with the exception of the Caprock Canyons Trailway, are short in length. Evidence of the success and value of rails-to-trails conversions can be found in the enthusiasm of the citizens of Quitaque and in the popularity of the Caprock Canyons Trailway. Call (202–797–5400) or write (1400 Sixteenth Street NW, Suite 300, Washington, DC 20036) the Rails-to-Trails Conservancy for more information about this worthwhile effort.

Outlined here is an out-and-back ride north from the trailhead of the Caprock Canyons Trailway in Quitaque into Caprock Canyon State Park. You'll encounter rugged canyon lands in the park, with some extraordinarily steep, but mercifully short, grades along the way. The park road is more likely to be traveled by pronghorn antelope and other animals than by automobiles.

There are other good roads to ride from Quitaque, but all require the ability to go long distances through remote country without stores for water and provisions. Ray Stark suggests a loop north toward Silverton and clockwise around the state park, returning through the town of Turkey. Tule Canyon near Lake MacKenzie and an extraordinary nine-mile stretch through the Palo Duro Canyon are worthy goals for very long rides out and back through open country to the northwest. There is also flatter terrain through the cotton fields to the south and east.

The Basics

Start: At the trailhead to the Caprock Canyons Trailway in Quitaque. Quitaque is about 100 miles southeast of Amarillo and 100 miles northeast of Lubbock.
Distance: 18.2 miles.

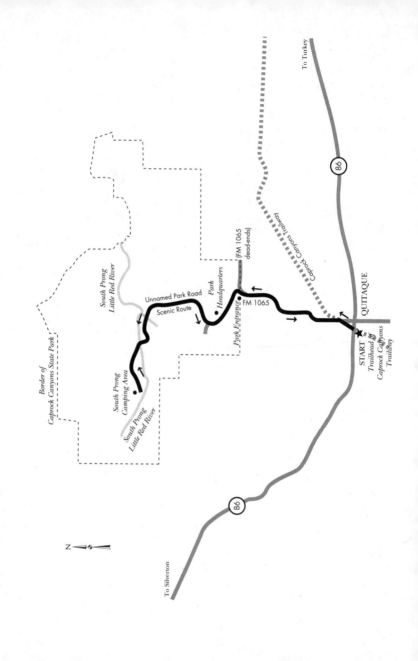

Terrain: Very steep—but short—grades through the canyon.
Roads: Quiet and isolated park road; little traffic on roads through Quitaque.
Food: Several options in Quitaque.

Miles & Directions

- 0.0 Leave the trailhead of the Caprock Canyons Trailway heading east on Texas 86.
- 0.2 Turn left (north) onto FM 1065 in Quitaque.
- 3.2 Bear left at the Y intersection toward the park entrance.
- 3.4 Enter Caprock Canyons State Park and cross cattle guard.
- 4.1 Pass park headquarters.
- 4.5 Take the right-hand turn directing you to "scenic route" and cross a cattle guard.
- 6.6 The road descends steeply into the canyon, with some steep, rolling grades along the way.
- 7.8 Cross South Prong of the Little Red River.
- 9.1 The road ends at the South Prong camping area. There is access to hiking trails, some parking, informational displays, and great views into the canyon here. Turn around and retrace your path along the park road to return to park headquarters.
- 13.7 At the T intersection, turn left toward the park entrance.
- 14.1 Pass park headquarters.
- 14.8 Cross cattle guard and exit park, bearing right onto FM 1065 (unmarked).
- 18.0 Turn right (west) onto Texas 86.
- 18.2 Finish at trailhead of Caprock Canyons Trailway.

45

Palo Duro Canyon Cruise

Palo Duro Canyon State Park

The approach to Palo Duro Canyon is an astonishing sight. The canyon is an immense natural wonder that appears very suddenly, seemingly out of nowhere.

The road toward the state park at Palo Duro Canyon passes through the flat, open pastureland of the Panhandle Plains. At the end of the road, suddenly and dramatically, the bottom drops out of the earth. The cover of the surrounding countryside is peeled off to expose a vast, almost indescribable interior. What was once an ordinary landscape instantly becomes a stunning and unique spectacle. There are few sights as beautiful and powerful, and it's hard to imagine so rapid a change in terrain.

Palo Duro Canyon was carved by the Prairie Dog Town Fork of the Red River. There are several crossings of this shallow river during the ride through the state park. Viewed close up, it seems unlikely that this river could have generated enough power to carve canyons so deep, thus suggesting the amount of time this work has been in process.

The total distance of this tour is relatively short, yet the climb out of the canyon is so long and steep that it's recommended only for cyclists who are physically fit and who have had climbing experience. The grade is rated at 10 percent for more than a mile, meaning that there is a one-foot rise in elevation for every ten linear feet of distance traveled. This translates into a drop of some 600 feet at the start of your ride. Some of the canyon walls rise 800 to 1,000 feet from the bottom. As much as you'll need leg strength and stamina to climb out of the canyon, you'll need bike handling skills on the descent to the canyon floor. Check your brakes and tires before beginning this ride.

An interesting historical marker at the park entrance recounts the establishment in the canyon of one of the largest cattle ranches in Texas. Another historical marker halfway into the ride describes earlier Indian settlement and battles. The park features other fascinating displays describing its geologic, cultural, and natural history, including a renowned outdoor theater presentation during summer evenings.

For a longer ride and to experience the dramatic effect of the approach to the canyon by bicycle, begin from the town square in Canyon, the same starting point as the **Panhandle Plains Challenge.** Take Texas 217 east from the town square for approximately thirteen miles to the park entrance. Texas 217 is part of the Texas Plains Trail, and it is completely exposed to the wind and elements. The contrast between these west Texas plains and the Palo Duro Canyon is profound.

The Basics

Start: At the entrance to Palo Duro Canyon State Park. The park is 12 miles east of Canyon, 25 miles southeast of Amarillo.
Distance: 15.3 miles. You can add additional laps of 5.1 miles on the park road at the bottom of the canyon. Starting at the town square in Canyon adds 13.1 miles in each direction on Texas 217 for a ride totaling 41.5 miles.
Terrain: The descent into and climb out of the canyon is rated at a 10 percent grade for 1.2 miles. Otherwise flat to gently rolling terrain.
Roads: Secluded park road with little traffic.
Food: Soda machine at park entrance; concessions in the park, including a restaurant, are open seasonally.

Miles & Directions

- 0.0 Head into the park on Park Rd. 5.

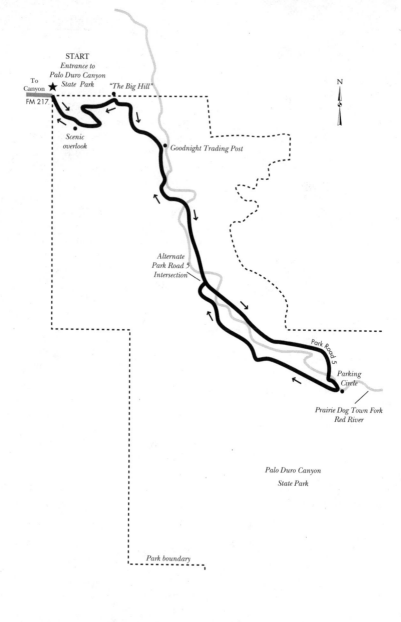

- 0.7 Pass a spectacular scenic overlook into the canyon.
- 1.6 Begin steep, twisting descent rated at 10 percent grade.
- 2.8 At bottom of descent, pass entrance to the Pioneer Amphitheater.
- 3.1 Goodnight Trading Post has vending machines and a restaurant open seasonally.
- 3.2 Pass Sad Monkey Scenic Railroad.
- 3.9 Pass rest rooms.
- 4.0 Water crossing #1.
- 5.0 Water crossing #2.
- 5.1 Continue straight past right-hand turn for Alternate Park Rd. 5. This is a loop.
- 5.4 Water crossing #3.
- 5.6 Water crossing #4.
- 5.9 Water crossing #5.
- 6.8 Pass restrooms.
- 7.6 The road bears right past a parking circle. At the beginning of an equestrian trail is a historical marker about the battle of Palo Duro Canyon.
- 7.7 Water crossing #6 is a spillway; be especially careful crossing.
- 10.2 At stop sign, turn left and retrace your steps to return to park entrance.

Turning right here allows you to ride additional laps through the park of 5.1 miles each.

- 10.3 Recross water crossing #2.
- 11.3 Recross water crossing #1. The 0.3-mile climb following this crossing is not the big one!
- 12.1 Pass Sad Monkey Scenic Railroad.
- 12.2 Pass Goodnight Trading Post.
- 12.5 Pass Pioneer Amphitheater and begin to climb.
- 13.7 Top of climb.
- 14.5 Pass scenic overlook.
- 15.3 Finish at park entrance.

46

Panhandle Plains Challenge

Canyon—Umbarger—
Buffalo Lake National Wildlife Refuge—Canyon

Canyon is a lovely college town just south of Amarillo. It is home to West Texas A & M University, where Nick Gerlich is a marketing professor. Nick also heads the Ultra Marathon Cycling Association, a national organization dedicated to long-distance bicycling.

Nick and his wife, Becky, have had some unique long-distance cycling adventures, including completing the Race Across America on a tandem bicycle. The Gerlichs have ridden on most of the roads in the Texas Panhandle while training for their long rides. They suggested this route, which starts in their hometown and passes through the west Texas plains.

This course passes through the wide open spaces of west Texas. With only a cursory glance, this countryside may strike you as plain and repetitive. Look closely, though, and you'll be surprised at the variety of life supported here.

The full tour passes through prime grazing land, a huge county feedlot, a national wildlife refuge, and the unique habitat of Prairie Dog Town, an undisturbed stretch of habitat for these unusual animals. Riders can cycle through one or more of these areas by choosing from four distance options. Be prepared for steady winds no matter what distance you select.

Leaving Canyon, the course heads north through some residential development and quickly enters open country. A turn to the west leads to the Randall County Feedyard. The feedlot can be quite a sight, with cattle as far as the eye can see. If the yard is full, and depending on the wind direction, you may be able to smell the feedlot long before you see it.

A shorter option bypasses the feedlot and heads straight into the countryside, where the feedlot's residents are raised. Here the pastureland is filled with cattle and horses grazing and roaming free in the fields. About halfway through the route is the town of Umbarger, where there is a store to resupply for the rest of your ride.

After leaving Umbarger, it is a short ride south to the Buffalo Lake National Wildlife Refuge. The character of the countryside changes only subtly as you approach the refuge, but the area's natural habitat is maintained so that it remains a winter haven for migrating ducks and geese. The refuge has popular interpretive trails for bird watchers, hikers, and motorists.

Just past the refuge entrance, you have another option to shorten your ride by turning east through ranch land. Continuing with the full tour takes you south past interpretive markers in Prairie Dog Town. The route then follows some very remote roads through miles of ranch land, home to more of the future occupants of the Randall County Feedyard. The ranch land past the refuge is quite flat, but you'll encounter some rolling terrain when the route turns north onto Soucy Road and heads back to Canyon.

The Basics

Start: At the town square in Canyon, corner of 15th St. and 4th Ave. Canyon is 10 miles south of Amarillo.

Distance: 55.3 miles, with shorter options of 45.3 miles, 40.5 miles, or 30.5 miles.

Terrain: Lots of flat, open, west Texas space. Some rolling hills through the Buffalo Lake National Wildlife Refuge and on Soucy Rd. on the return to Canyon.

Roads: FM roads are two lanes, no shoulder, and lightly traveled. Roads to the north of Canyon have more traffic than those to the south, some of which are quite isolated. If you choose the shorter options, US 60 has high-speed traffic but a wide shoulder.

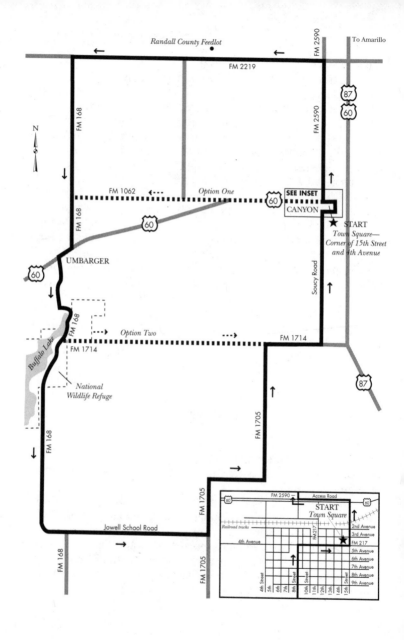

Food: Lots of options in Canyon; convenience store in Umbarger. Take plenty of water if you ride the full tour.

Miles & Directions

- 0.0 From the town square at the corner of 15th St. and 4th Ave., head north on 15th St.
- 0.2 Cross railroad tracks.
- 0.4 After crossing overpass over US 60, turn left onto the access road.

For a shorter option of 45.3 miles that misses the Randall County Feedyard, turn left on US 60, which has high-speed traffic but a wide shoulder (or stay on the access road, which parallels US 60 for 2.5 miles, and then get on US 60). At mile 4.0 turn right (west) onto FM 1062. At mile 10.0 turn left (south) onto FM 168 and follow the directions for the full tour from mile 20.0.

- 0.8 Turn right (north) onto FM 2590. Two lanes, narrow shoulder, open country.
- 5.9 At stop sign, turn left (west) onto FM 2219. Adequate narrow shoulder.
- 10.0 Pass the Randall County Feedyard.
- 14.9 Bear left where the road intersects with a small feeder road and becomes FM 168. Wide, open spaces, with cows, horses, and barbed wire fences on the horizon.
- 20.0 Continue straight past stop sign junction of FM 1062.
- 21.9 Turn right as FM 168 merges with US 60. Wide shoulder, high-speed traffic.
- 22.2 Enter Umbarger, pass town sign and convenience store.
- 22.4 Carefully turn left across traffic and railroad tracks to continue south on FM 168.
- 24.4 Road curves left past entrance to Buffalo Lake National Wildlife Refuge. Follow main road into small canyon, past dam.
- 25.8 Continue past junction of FM 1714 to the left.

For a shorter option of 40.5 miles that misses Prairie Dog Town, turn left (east) onto FM 1714, immediately encountering a small climb. After 7.4 miles you'll pass the intersection of FM 1705. Continue straight on FM 1714 and follow directions for the full tour from mile 48.1 to return to Canyon. If you also chose the shorter option that misses the Randall County Feedyard, your ride will total 30.5 miles.

- 27.2 Pass markers to the left describing Prairie Dog Town; terrain is a little more rolling through the refuge, past mostly open and empty country. Visibility straight ahead for a long way.
- 33.8 Continue straight onto the Jowell School Rd. as FM 168 veers to the right.
- 39.1 At stop sign and radio tower, turn left onto FM 1705 (unmarked).
- 41.0 Follow paved road to the right.
- 42.9 Confusing intersection here. Bear left to stay on main road, which intersects with another unmarked paved road.
- 48.1 At stop sign intersection, turn right (east) onto FM 1714. Two lanes, no shoulder.
- 50.1 Turn left (north) onto Soucy Rd. If you come to US 87 you've gone 1 mile too far. Soucy Rd. has some rolling terrain.
- 52.6 Cross railroad tracks. Soucy Rd. becomes 8th St. in town. Pass convenience store and Canyon High School.
- 54.8 At stop sign, turn right onto 4th Ave.
- 55.3 Finish at the town square.

47

Davis Mountains Classic

Fort Davis—McDonald Observatory—
Skillman's Grove—Fort Davis

This spectacular tour follows a course known locally only as the Scenic Loop. The Scenic Loop provides one of the most dramatic and challenging bicycle routes in Texas. Virtually the entire ride takes place at an altitude higher than a mile, with views toward some of the state's highest mountain peaks. A two-mile side road on Mount Locke leading to the McDonald Observatory ends at the highest point on Texas highways.

The Scenic Loop passes through countryside containing all the variety west Texas has to offer. This is a tour of beautiful vistas that include mountain passes, deep canyons, open range, and hilly pastures. Abundant wildlife is in evidence throughout the year, and herds of mule deer, pronghorn antelope, and wild boars are used to having these roads to themselves.

One thing the Scenic Loop doesn't have once you leave town and pass the state park is a place to buy provisions. Other than the observatory visitors center, there isn't even a place to fill a water bottle. Riders on this course should be supported, or fully self-sufficient, for food and spare parts.

The route begins in historic Fort Davis, which was established as an army outpost to protect early pioneers drawn west by the California gold rush. The fort is preserved by the National Park Service. Just out of town, after riding through beautiful Limpia Canyon, you'll pass the Davis Mountains State Park with the restored Indian Lodge; both are wonderfully maintained by Texas Parks and

Wildlife. Be sure to make reservations well in advance if you hope to stay at the lodge.

Glimpses of the McDonald Observatory high atop Mount Locke appear in the distance as the route heads into the mountains. After passing a field of solar panels, there are 3.5 miles of almost continuous climbing before the road levels out just before the turn to the observatory. Be sure to pace yourself; there are plenty of hills to follow. There is a rest stop with a terrific view about halfway up this climb.

A side trip to tour the observatory should be mandatory for anyone visiting the Fort Davis area. If you tackle this portion of Mount Locke by bicycle, be prepared for a grade rated at an extraordinary 17 percent for almost two miles.

Past the observatory the road winds, dips, rises, and falls for miles through wooded hills and mountain pastures. After a wonderful descent out of the mountains and onto grassy plains, the road continues for five relatively flat miles straight toward Sawtooth Mountain. There is more climbing and descending to come through this surprising Texas range.

Eventually the course leaves the protection of the mountains for good and travels back to Fort Davis through open pastureland and grazing land. This expanse is broken briefly by Skillman's Grove, a shaded site that for more than a century has been used only for religious retreats in summer.

Ed Barker cycled these roads during the three years he spent in Fort Davis as superintendent of the observatory. He notes that some of the conditions that make this location so good for the observatory—like clear skies, high altitudes, and restrictions on development—pose special challenges for cyclists. Temperatures plummet rapidly toward sunset, dehydration is accelerated in the thin air, and assistance is often far away.

Leaving the roadway to venture into the countryside also can prove problematic. Private property rights are fiercely protected, and poisonous animals inhabit parts of this rugged land. Rattlesnakes are especially fond of the warmth of the pavement in spring and fall. Make use of the many public rest stops and picnic areas along the way when you need a break.

Although remotely located, this is a special route with unique challenges. The Permian Basin Cycling Association hosts a popular, well-supported event at the end of September, an especially good time of year to try this classic ride. Check with the association and with the Prude Ranch for other organized cycling activities along the Scenic Loop.

The Basics

Start: In Fort Davis, in front of the Jeff Davis County courthouse. There is public parking around the courthouse and in the town square. Fort Davis is about 600 miles west of Houston and 150 miles southwest of Midland.

Distance: 75.4 miles.

Terrain: First half is mountainous; second half is flat to slightly rolling.

Roads: Two-lane state roads have shoulders up to the McDonald Observatory but no shoulders thereafter. Past the observatory, traffic is very light. This can be a very isolated route.

Food: The observatory visitors center, which closes at 5:00 P.M., has a water fountain and vending machines inside. There are several options in Fort Davis, but you must otherwise be self-sufficient along this route. Because of altitude and dry air, you may need to drink more than usual.

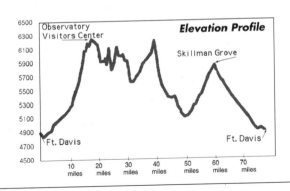

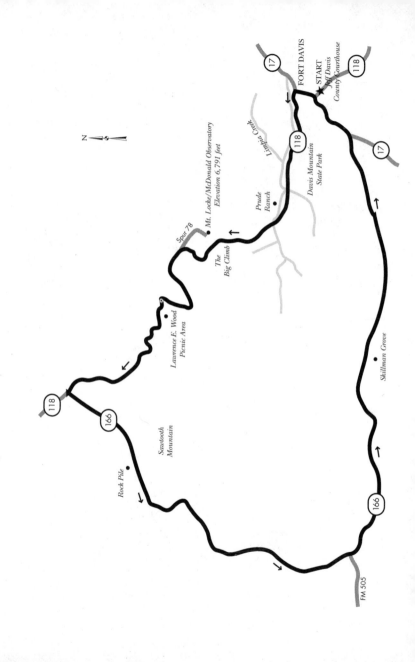

Miles & Directions

- 0.0 Head north on Texas 17/Texas 118 through town.
- 0.8 Pass entrance to Fort Davis National Historic Site. Restored Fort Davis is clearly visible to the left, at the base of the cliffs known as the Sleeping Lion Formation.
- 1.5 Stay on Texas 118 by bearing left as Texas 17 diverges to the right, and begin to climb through beautiful tree-lined Limpia Canyon. Road has wide shoulder.
- 4.1 Pass Park Rd. 3 to the left, the entrance to Davis Mountains State Park and Indian Lodge.
- 5.7 Pass entrance to Prude Ranch.
- 10.3 Pass a solar park, a utility solar-generation project with hundreds of solar panels.
- 11.0 The big climb begins. Pace yourself; there is a short reprieve at mile 12.5, but you climb for a total of 3.5 miles.
- 12.7 Especially steep part of climb begins.
- 13.4 Picnic area rest stop.
- 15.4 Pass junction of Spur 78, the road to the observatory. The visitors center is 0.2 mile on the right.

It's another 1.6 miles to the observatory at the top of Mt. Locke, which is graded at an incredible 17 percent. There's no climbing to reach the nearby visitors center.

- 16.8 Cattle guard. Lots of ups and downs to come.
- 21.5 Cattle guard on a downhill, loose livestock nearby.
- 23.4 Cattle guard on a downhill.
- 23.9 Pass Lawrence E. Wood picnic area, no water here.
- 24.5 Cattle guard.
- 29.6 At the Y intersection, bear left (south) onto Texas 166 following the signs to Fort Davis. The rock formation you're heading toward in the distance is Sawtooth Mountain.
- 35.6 Pass an unusual rock pile—a huge stack of boulders—on the left. It's fenced off on land privately owned.

- 38.8 Cattle guard on a downhill.
- 39.4 Pass a picnic table and rest stop.
- 42.3 Cross particularly bad cattle guard.
- 46.9 Cattle guard; terrain becomes flat and open for a long stretch.
- 49.8 Stay straight on Texas 166 south past the intersection of FM 505 to the right. There are at least seven cattle guard crossings in the next 11 miles.
- 52.3 Cross a particularly bad cattle guard.
- 53.1 Pass Battle Springs ranch and enter some hillier terrain.
- 56.2 Cross a particularly bad cattle guard.
- 59.1 Historical marker in front of Bloys Camp, a religious retreat since the 1850s. You can see the cluster of tin buildings in Skillman Grove from a distance. Retreat is used only in summer. Leaving Skillman Grove, the terrain is flat and open into Fort Davis.
- 63.7 Pass picnic area.
- 73.0 Turn left (north) at yield intersection onto Texas 17. Two wide lanes, pavement is a little rougher.
- 75.1 Pass Fort Davis High School.
- 75.3 Stay left on Texas 17 as it combines with Texas 118 north; Texas 118 south veers right.
- 75.4 Finish at Jeff Davis County courthouse.

48

Giant Classic

Fort Davis—Alpine—Marfa—Fort Davis

A wonderful movie starring James Dean, Elizabeth Taylor, and Rock Hudson chronicles west Texas life after the discovery of oil. *Giant* was filmed in the countryside near Marfa, and long stretches of this route pass through the ranch land and oil fields that provided the backdrop for this film classic.

The images in the movie are often of a desolate, sparsely populated part of the country. To be sure, there is lots of land supporting a small population here. Over half of the ride takes place in Brewster County, the largest of Texas's 254 counties. Brewster County is larger than the states of Connecticut and Rhode Island combined.

There is much more to see on this route than the empty spaces of the Marfa Basin. These are open roads, but the expanse of the west Texas countryside is punctuated by some unique geology. Among other things, this route circumscribes a prehistoric volcanic center, whose influences are still visible all along the way.

Begin your ride at the Jeff Davis County courthouse in Fort Davis, using the same starting point as the **Davis Mountains Classic.** Across the street is the Limpia Hotel, a beautifully restored hotel furnished in the style of its turn-of-the-century origin. Heading south from Fort Davis, the route passes over arid plains toward the Chihuahuan Desert Visitors Center and then drops into exotic Musquiz Canyon. The roads that cut through the canyon display the first evidence of the prehistoric lava flows and volcanic activity responsible for the area's geology.

After dropping out of the mountains, you'll cross open plains to Alpine, past the distinctive natural landmarks of Barillos Dome and Mitre Peak in the distance. Alpine is the seat of Brewster County and home of Sul Ross University. This small town is a popular recreational center because of its climate and proximity to the mountains.

From Alpine you'll turn west on a long, steady climb through the remains of the Paisano Volcano, active thirty-five million years ago and still the dominant geological feature of this area. The roads that cut along this portion of the route expose the internal workings of this volcano, recorded in the layers and formations of broken and fragmented rock, granite, and lava flows it left behind.

Halfway to Marfa you'll reach the top of this climb at the Paisano Pass, which was first crossed by Spanish explorers in the sixteenth century. This pass became a well-known spot on the Chihuahuan Trail to California during the years of the gold rush. The railroad track paralleling the path of this trail is still a main line to the west.

Descending from the pass, you'll head into the Marfa Basin and the land of *Giant*. On the way is a viewing area for the Marfa Mystery Lights, Marfa's most famous attraction. The lights are an unexplained natural phenomenon that are visible only at night. Just before entering Marfa you'll cross the Presidio County line, which is marked by an interesting historical marker claiming the county seat at Presidio, some sixty miles south, as the oldest town in America and sight of the first recorded wagon train crossing into Texas in 1582. Presidio is also the halfway point of the **El Camino del Rio Classic** .

Turning north in Marfa, the road crosses Alamito Creek and more of the terrain of the Marfa Basin reminiscent of the movie *Giant*. There is some rise in elevation as you pass through the desert flats at the edge of the Davis Mountains to finish your ride in Fort Davis.

Preparation for long outdoor exposure is essential on this route. There are virtually no shaded stretches, and services are available only in the towns at the corners of this triangular tour. Because of the high altitude and clear skies, there can be wide variances in the daily temperature, strong sun, and rapid changes in the weather. Drink more than you normally would when riding, and bring extra sunscreen and wind protection.

The Basics

Start: In Fort Davis at the Jeff Davis County courthouse, at the corner of Texas 17 and Texas 118. There is parking around the courthouse and the adjacent town square. Fort Davis is 500 miles southwest of Dallas and 200 miles east of El Paso.

Distance: 71.4 miles.

Terrain: Many wide, open, exposed stretches. Some gradual climbing and descending close to Fort Davis. A long gradual climb from Alpine to the Paisano Pass.

Roads: All roads have wide shoulders. Texas 17 and Texas 118 are lightly traveled. There is heavier traffic on US 67/US 90.

Food: Several options in Fort Davis, Alpine, and Marfa, but nothing in between.

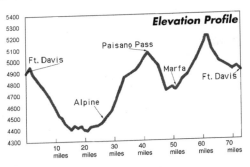

Miles & Directions

- 0.0 Begin south (left) on Texas 118, marked as the Texas Mountain Trail.
- 4.2 Pass entrance to Chihuahuan Desert Visitors Center. Historical marker and ruins of the ranch home of Manuel

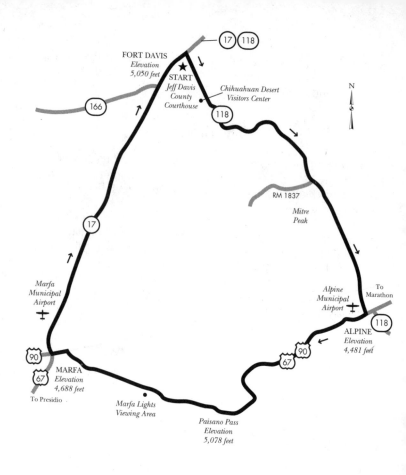

Musquiz, early pioneer for whom the surrounding canyon is named, is at mile 6.2.

- 6.6 Pass entrance to Calamity Creek Ranch and head toward interesting stone formations.
- 10.5 Pass historical marker for the first rural school west of the Pecos River, built in 1881.
- 13.9 Continue straight past junction of RM 1837 to the right. From here to Alpine is flat and open and exposed to the elements.
- 15.2 Cross Brewster County line.
- 21.6 Pass Alpine Municipal Airport to the right.
- 21.7 Cross railroad tracks.
- 22.7 Pass Alpine town sign. Texas 118 becomes North 5th Street in town.
- 23.5 Pass convenience store.
- 23.8 At stop sign intersection, turn right (west) onto US 67/US 90; one-way traffic here. Note a variety of stores, bakeries, and restaurants, and the Brewster County courthouse to the left of this turn.
- 24.5 Cross railroad tracks.
- 24.8 Pass convenience store. Some traffic through town. After leaving town, begin a long climb toward Paisano Pass. Higher-speed traffic; shoulder narrows to accommodate climbing lanes at some points.
- 37.3 Historical marker at top of Paisano Pass, with views of the high plains, open and filled with tumbleweed. Pass viewing area for Marfa Mystery Lights at mile 41.3. Pass historical marker at Presidio County line at mile 49.2.
- 49.8 Pass Marfa town sign and first of several convenience stores.
- 50.2 Turn right (north) onto Texas 17 at traffic light, also called Highland.
- 50.3 Cross railroad tracks.
- 50.4 Continue on Texas 17 by following signs to right, and then immediately left, around the very prominent Presidio County courthouse. Texas 17 is also called Dean St. here.
- 54.4 Pass Marfa Municipal Airport. Potential for continuing

construction and patches of rough road throughout this stretch.

- 69.0 Pass intersection of Texas 166 to the left.
- 71.1 Pass Fort Davis High School.
- 71.3 Stay left on Texas 17 as it combines with Texas 118 north; Texas 118 south veers right.
- 71.4 Finish at Jeff Davis County courthouse.

49

Two Chisos
Mountain Challenges

*Big Bend National Park—Chisos Basin—Panther
Junction—Rio Grande Village—Boquillas Canyon*

Big Bend National Park occupies 1,100 square miles along the Mexican border of west Texas, where the southern flow of the Rio Grande bends abruptly north. It's impossible to catalog all the variety and contrast contained in this vast area. Visitors could spend a lifetime exploring among the spectacular canyons of the Rio Grande, the unique natural features in the Chihuahuan Desert, and the majestic formations of the Chisos Mountains, all of which are contained in the park.

Bike routes out-and-back along thirty-five miles of park roads, which traverse portions of the park's canyons, desert, and mountains, are described here. Between the two ends of these roads is a 4,000-foot change in elevation. A round-trip from either end combines an almost unbroken descent with one of the most arduous climbs to be found in Texas. Starting in the middle at the park's main visitors center allows for two dramatic Challenges in Texas's most celebrated national park.

The list of cautions the National Park Service presents to visitors is quite comprehensive. Take heed of their advice, and make special preparations for a long ride through the wilderness of Big Bend. Desert heat requires that you drink plenty of water, cover yourself from the sun and wind, and time your ride before or after the heat of midday. Unusual wildlife including poisonous snakes, scorpions, and larger wild animals inhabit the park. Higher altitudes feature thin air and changing temperatures. Be well prepared mentally and physically, and if you're traveling alone, let someone know where you're going and when you expect to return.

Both of these Challenges leave from the Panther Junction visitors center inside the park. The first option drops 2,000 feet in elevation as it travels southeast through the plains of the Chihuahuan Desert to the Rio Grande. At the river, a magnificent five-mile side road climbs through Boquillas Canyon, one of the park's three huge canyons carved by the Rio Grande. There is a terrific hiking trail into Boquillas Canyon, which is seventeen miles long and up to 1,500 feet deep. There is a visitors center and store at the end of the road in the Rio Grande Village, where you can resupply for the long climb back to Panther Junction.

The second option rises more than 2,000 feet in elevation as it travels southwest into the Chisos Mountains. The ride is breathtaking, both figuratively and literally, as you climb into the heart of this daunting range. After the climb peaks, the road plummets another mile into the Chisos Basin, where there is a renowned lodge and a well-supplied store.

You're sure to take a long rest in the beautiful mountain basin after the effort of your ride to the top. This will make the one-mile climb out of the basin on your return all the more challenging. Once you've crested this climb, though, the only effort you'll exert the rest of the way to Panther Junction will be an occasional touch of your brakes to slow a superb descent.

The Basics

Start: At the Panther Junction Visitor Center and Park Headquarters in the Big Bend National Park. The park headquarters is about 80 miles south of Marathon and 140 miles southeast of Fort Davis.
Distance: Southeast to the Rio Grande Village is 40.8 miles round-trip (48.0 miles including a side trip to Boquillas Canyon). Southwest to the Chisos Basin is 19.2 miles round-trip.

Terrain: Southeast to the Rio Grande Village is a long descent through the Chihuahuan Desert. Side trip to Boquillas Canyon is hilly. Southwest to the Chisos Basin is an extraordinarily long and steep climb.

Roads: Two-lane park roads with no shoulder. Traffic is light, but RVs and campers are prominent.

Food: Water and restrooms at all three visitors centers. Service station near Panther Junction has some supplies. Well-stocked stores near the visitors centers at the end of the roads in Rio Grande Village and Chisos Basin.

Miles & Directions

Option One (southeast to the Rio Grande Village)

- 0.0 Exit Panther Junction visitors center by turning right on the unnamed park road toward Rio Grande Village. Two lanes, no shoulder. What little traffic there is includes RVs and campers.

  The first 3 miles roll slightly upward, with views into the plains of the Chihuahuan Desert to the left and the Chisos Mountains to the right.

- 3.4 Begin a steady downhill through open desert for almost 13 miles.
- 5.4 Pass Glen Springs Rd. (dirt) to the right.
- 6.4 Pass dirt road to Dugout Wells to the left.
- 14.0 An interesting change in the character of the road along a short, rolling, twisty section.
- 15.7 Pass River Rd. East (dirt) to the right after nice descent and vista.
- 16.1 After crossing a bridge, begin to climb.
- 16.9 Pass road to Hot Springs (dirt) on right.
- 18.0 Pass Old Ore Rd. (dirt) to the left.
- 18.5 Crest climb and begin a descent through a short tunnel.

MEXICO

Rio Grande

Boquillas Canyon
Overlook

Rio Grande
overlook

Rio Grande Village
(Elevation 1,850 ft.)

Hot Springs
Road (dirt)

Rio Grande

Park Road
(unnamed)

Option One

Glen Springs
Road (dirt)

N

Park Road
to Marathon

385

Option
Two

START
Panther Junction
Visitor Center
(Elevation 3,750 ft.)

Park Road
to Terlingua

118

Chisos Mountain Lodge
(Elevation 5,401 ft.)

- 18.7 Exit tunnel and pass Rio Grande Overlook.
- 19.4 Pass paved road to the left leading to Boquillas, Mexico, and to Boquillas Canyon Overlook.

For a magnificent addition to Boquillas Canyon totaling 7.2 miles, turn left onto this road, which begins winding uphill. After 1.4 miles, pass the road crossing to Boquillas, Mexico, to the right and begin another twisted, steeper climb with some dramatic views into the mountains. After 2.7 miles, pass a paved road to Boquillas Canyon Overlook (the overlook is 0.5 mile from this intersection). After 3.6 miles, the road ends at a parking area with a hiking trail leading into Boquillas Canyon. Retrace your path on this road to resume the full tour.

- 20.2 Pass Rio Grande Village visitors center.
- 20.4 Road ends at Rio Grande Village Store. Retrace your path to return to the Panther Junction visitors center.
- 22.2 After a short climb and passage through the tunnel, the road turns downhill briefly.
- 25.1 After crossing bridge, pass River Rd. East and begin the long climb back to Panther Junction.
- 35.4 Pass Glen Springs Rd. (dirt) to the left.
- 40.8 Finish at Panther Junction visitors center.

Option Two (southwest to the Chisos Basin)

- 0.0 Exit Panther Junction visitors center by turning left on the unnamed park road. Uphill grade, two lanes, no shoulder.

The first 3 miles are on an uphill grade, with views into the plains of the Chihuahuan Desert to the right and the Chisos Mountains to the left.

- 0.2 Pass Panther Junction Service Station and store to the left.
- 3.2 Turn left at sign directing you to the Chisos Basin.

The next 5 miles are all uphill into the mountains, with magnificent views all the way. There are several roadside pulloffs for cars that also make good rest stops. As you climb, the road becomes steeper and the thin air becomes cooler.

- 8.3 Top of the climb, just before the parking area for Lost Mine Trail. A very steep, twisting descent to the basin follows with more gorgeous views.
- 9.4 Continue straight past entrance to campground and amphitheater to the right.
- 9.6 Road ends at visitors center and Chisos Mountain Lodge. There is a store here, along with hiking trails and nice views. Retrace your path on this road to return to Panther Junction.
- 10.9 Top of steep climb past parking lot for Lost Mine Trail; beginning of a 5-mile descent.
- 16.0 At the bottom of the mountain, at the T intersection, turn right on the unnamed park road.
- 19.2 Finish at Panther Junction visitors center.

50

El Camino del Rio Classic

Big Bend Ranch State Natural Area—Lajitas—
Redford—Fort Leaton—Presidio—
Big Bend Ranch State Natural Area

This ride traces a remotely located out-and-back route along a road acclaimed as one of the most spectacular in Texas. The Rio Grande forms the border between Texas and Mexico. El Camino del Rio, the "River Road," runs parallel to the river for most of the fifty miles between the small border towns of Lajitas and Presidio.

Lajitas was established in 1915 as a U.S. army outpost to protect the Big Bend area from border crossings by Pancho Villa during the Mexican Revolution. Presidio was established in the sixteenth century as a Spanish army outpost at the location of the first crossings from Mexico into the Texas territories. A storied trail developed over the rugged and barren mountain country between these two outposts.

Because distances are great and services are few, supported multi-day tours are a popular way to see this part of Texas by bicycle. Since there are so few roads, the few loops that can be fashioned through southwest Texas must cover hundreds of miles. Commercial bicycle tour companies, such as Lawrence Walker's Coyote Bicycle Tours, offer expertise and guidance for an even more ambitious bike ride in this area. You can write Lawrence at P.O. Box 1832, Austin, Texas 78767, for more information about supported multiday tours throughout Texas.

Lajitas is the Spanish word for flagstones, and the town bills itself as "not really near anywhere." These descriptions will be evident as you begin your ride and continue through the rocky and remote mountains and canyons along the river's edge. Lajitas is headquarters for a popular and well-attended mountain bike festival held each February. There are organized rides, races, exhibitions, and unusual events on and off the road around Lajitas, toward nearby Terlingua, and across the river to San Carlos, Mexico.

Most of El Camino del Rio is contained in a recently formed state park, the Big Bend Ranch State Natural Area. This ride starts at park headquarters a mile east of Lajitas. El Camino del Rio is the only paved road between Lajitas and Presidio, but many wilderness trails and dirt roads are gradually being opened in this immense state park.

Steep grades, sharp curves, and low-water crossings will test your cycling skills on this Classic ride, especially over the first twenty miles. You can fashion an out-and-back ride of any distance along El Camino del Rio, but at a minimum try to ride to the big hill at mile 14. This hill is rated at a 15 percent grade for almost a mile, making it the steepest regularly traveled grade on Texas highways. (The spur road to the McDonald Observatory, on the **Davis Mountains Classic**, is rated at a 17 percent grade.) The views in both directions of the Rio Grande from the top of this hill are well worth the effort.

A ride past the big hill toward Presidio continues across creeks and canyons, past unusual rock formations, and into farmland and ranch land. Past the small town of Redford is another state park facility containing historic Fort Leaton. An interesting historical marker recounts the history of generations of conflict between Spanish, Indian, and Anglo inhabitants.

Texas Parks and Wildlife runs a guided bus tour (available by reservation) between the Big Bend Ranch State Natural Area park headquarters in Lajitas and the park at Fort Leaton. Unfortunately, there are no commercial bus services to take you and your bicycle back to Lajitas from Presidio if you've made it this far. It's only a short distance further from Fort Leaton to Presidio but a long way retracing your steps back to Lajitas. As with many out-and-back rides, though, the landscape along El Camino del Rio is so rich and unique that a ride in the opposite direction seems like a different ride entirely.

The Basics

Start: At the Barton Warnock Environmental Education Center of the Big Bend Ranch State Natural Area near Lajitas. Lajitas is 40 miles west of the Panther Junction park headquarters for the Big Bend National Park.

Distance: 100.0 miles out and back. Any shorter out-and-back option is available, but at least a 30-mile round-trip to the top of the climb of the 15 percent grade is recommended.

Terrain: Rolling, mountainous terrain, leveling off somewhat on the approach to Presidio.

Roads: This route is all on one road, FM 170. Two lanes, no shoulder, little traffic.

Food: Limited choices in Lajitas, Redford, and Presidio.

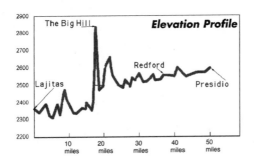

Miles & Directions

- 0.0 Exit the Barton Warnock Environmental Education Center of the Big Bend Ranch State Natural Area by turning left onto FM 170.
- 1.1 Pass Lajitas town sign and climb into town, past the western storefronts and businesses offering horse rides and river

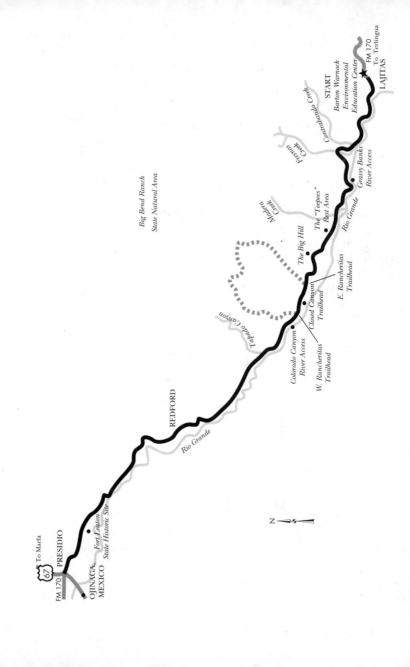

tours. There are limited choices for accommodations and food in town.

- 2.0 Enter Presidio County and continue parallel to the Rio Grande. The road follows increasingly steeper rolling terrain.
- 6.4 Cross Contrabando Creek. Road alternately follows and pulls away from river. Hardscrabble character of the countryside continues.
- 7.8 Cross Fresnos Creek.
- 10.3 After turning back toward the river for a while, cross a big climb and drop.
- 10.7 Grassy Banks, access point to the Rio Grande, to the left; dirt road, wilderness camping.
- 13.0 Pass another river camping access; dirt road.
- 13.3 Cross Madera Creek. Note warnings for low-water crossings.
- 13.7 Pass the "teepees" highway rest area. Note sign warning of rock slides. Begin steep and breathtaking climb past field of boulders.

The climb to come is rated at a 15 percent grade in each direction.

- 14.7 Top of the climb, with famous views down the river in each direction.
- 19.9 Pass E. Rancheritas trailhead to the right, a wilderness hiking trail through the state park.
- 21.3 Pass Closed Canyon trailhead to the left.
- 22.7 Pass W. Rancheritas trailhead to the right.
- 23.1 Pass Colorado Canyon access to Rio Grande, near a very pretty river section.
- 26.3 Cross Tapado Canyon.
- 26.7 Begin half-mile stretch of road with some tree and cliff cover.
- 30.2 Pass private residences.
- 35.1 Pass Redford town sign.
- 36.1 Pass Redford convenience store.
- 36.6 Cross cattle guard.
- 38.7 Cross cattle guard.

- 40.8 Cross cattle guard.
- 43.7 Pass dirt road for Casa Piedra to the right.
- 45.0 Cross Alamita Creek.
- 47.8 Pass Fort Leaton.
- 48.4 Pass Presidio town sign. FM 170 is the only paved road in town for a while.
- 50.0 Turn around at Presidio High School. There is a convenience store across the street. Retrace your path on FM 170 to return to Lajitas.

1.5 miles further along on FM 170 into town are more stores and a restaurant. The border town of Ojinaga, Mexico, has more interesting places to eat.

- 62.9 Pass convenience store in Redford.
- 85.3 Top of climb of 15 percent grade.
- 100.0 Finish at Barton Warnock Center.

Appendix A

They're Just CALLED Centuries

by Maynard Hershon

I love riding centuries. I always intend to ride several each season and end up doing only a few. If you're a racer or gnarly mountain bikin' dude, you may think centuries are for wimps or "poppy-watchers," well, that's your loss: centuries are fun.

If you've never ridden a century, here's what it's like. You travel (probably, sigh, by car) to a place, most likely a scenic place, where you do not normally go.

You park the car early on a weekend morning and stand in line a few minutes to register; costs a modest amount of money. Maybe you pay a little extra for the souvenir T-shirt, better looking this year than last, but not as neat as the one from '92.

Then you unload your trusty ol' Murray or Merlin ten-speed and ride it 30, 50, 65, 100 or 125 miles, whatever you feel like. They're just CALLED centuries—you don't have to ride 100 miles. The nice folks at registration will give you a route map or you can simply obey the color-coded arrows painted on the road. No worries: hardly anyone gets lost. For long.

Remember, the routes you're riding are the finest the cyclists in that area (the scenic one to which you would not normally go) can provide for your pedaling pleasure. They're proud of their area and their roads, and they'd like you to be impressed too. Note: With your newfound knowledge you can, at your option, return to that area and ride those roads again, without benefit of registration, map or color-coded arrows. No one will mind, but you will not receive a souvenir T-shirt.

As you ride the century, every so often you stop and snag food from tables heavy-laden with food. You get cold drinks from icy-

cold coolers on tables nearby, equally heavy-laden with coolers. Sports drinks, lemonade, iced tea and water are typical choices. If you ride 65 miles, my favorite distance, you may stop, oh, three times for food (newtons, maybe, bananas, chocolate chip cookies, peanut butter/jelly sands, orange sections) and liquid.

If, say, you demand maximum effectiveness from your tough weekend morning workouts, you can ride right by all the roadside rest stops, featuring, as they do, that tasty food and those cold drinks. Suit yourself. Most people, honestly, do not ride right by. They stop, take off their helmets, eat and drink. Sometimes, as they eat and drink, they sit on the grass under shade trees in informal sweaty groups. Some remove cycling shoes. They stretch out their legs on the grass and chat with one another about how good the food tastes and how cold the drinks are. Perhaps you've just eaten as you read this. You have to imagine how good that food tastes and how pleasant it is to down about a gallon of icy-cold lemonade—after, oh, fifty 90-degree miles.

Any of this century stuff sound objectionable so far? No? As I said, I like riding 100 kilometers, about 65 miles. Sixty-five miles seems like a real ride—but I can still stay awake later in the day when, feet up on the couch, frosty can of electrolyte replacement fluid in hand, I listen to my non-riding wife tell me how HER morning went. Sure enough, riding the distance, enjoying the good roads and the food and drink are important parts of the century experience. But here's (sound of trumpets) the best part. While you're out there on those roads, hundreds of other folks are out there too. Same roads, same morning. Hundreds of cycling persons you don't know.

You can talk to them. It's easy if you use this proven technique. First, pick a person: use any criteria you judge appropriate. Then—check traffic behind you. Wait until the road is free of traffic. Then simply adjust your gear selection and pedaling cadence until you and the person with whom you wish to converse are traveling at the same speed. Next—align your bicycle with that person's in the road, front wheel next to front wheel, rear wheel next to rear, either on the right side or the left, maybe two feet away. Once you've done that, you'll find that you and that individual are side-by-side in the road, spaced apart a convenient distance for spoken communication.

Merely say hi. Smile, maybe. If that person responds, and you respond to their response, and they respond once again—YOU've got a conversation going. Actual human contact. Sounds easy, doesn't it? Try it. It works nearly every time.

I love riding centuries.

Maynard Hershon is a renowned chronicler of cycling experiences. He is a columnist and senior writer for VeloNews *and has published two popular anthologies of his stories, "Tales from the Bike Shop" and "Half Wheel Hell."*

Appendix B

Calendar of Organized Rides and Cycling Events

Some of the best bike rides in Texas are organized events. Civic and charitable groups across the state sponsor bike rides throughout the year, sometimes in the most unlikely of places and at the most unlikely of times.

With his unique insight and style, Maynard Hershon chronicles the advantages and benefits of participating in an organized event in his commentary "They're Just CALLED Centuries." Riders of all levels of experience and ability can benefit from an organized ride and will relate to Maynard's experiences.

With the increasing popularity of cycling in Texas and the demonstrated success of organized tours as vehicles for fund-raising and promoting tourism, a growing number of events have found their way onto the Texas cycling calendar. This appendix lists many, but not all, of these events. If you have a favorite event not listed here, or if you know of changes to the dates, descriptions, and contact telephone numbers listed, I'd be glad to receive updated information for inclusion in future editions of this book. Write to me in care of the publisher or by "e-mail" at txbikebook@aol.com.

Central Texas and the Hill Country

April
- Burnet Bluebonnet Festival Tour, Burnet. (512) 756–4297.
- Easter Hill Country Tour, Kerrville. Three days. (713) 935–2810.
- Great Austin to Shiner Pedal (GASP), Austin. (512) 474–9092.

- Kids to Camp, College Station. Sponsored by the College Station Noon Lions. (409) 696–9102.
- MS 150 Bike Tour, Houston to Austin. Benefits the Multiple Sclerosis Society, two-day tour. (713) 526–8967 or (800) 323–4873.
- Redbud Road Rally, Goldthwaite. (915) 648–2216.

May

- Armadillo Hill Country Classic, Austin. (512) 477–0776.
- Clean Air Challenge, Austin. Benefits the American Lung Association. (512) 346–9308 or (800) 252–5864.
- Ride for Sight, Giddings. Sponsored by the Giddings Lions Club. (409) 542–3446.

June

- CASA Break the Cycle Bike-a-thon, Austin. Benefits Child Advocacy Services of Austin. (512) 443–2272.

September

- Tour de Bastrop, Bastrop. Benefits the Bastrop Opera House. (512) 321–6283.

October

- October Cycling Fest, Fredericksburg. Sponsored by Hill Country Memorial Hospital Wellness Center. (210) 997–1355.
- Outlaw Trail 100, Round Rock. Sponsored by Round Rock Parks and Recreation Department. (512) 255–5147.
- Pflugerville Pumpkin Pflyer, Pflugerville. (512) 251–5082.
- Power Pedal, Bryan. Sponsored by Bryan Utilities. (409) 821–5772.
- Waco Wild West Century, Waco. (817) 772–7150.
- Wimberley Hillaceous, Wimberley. Sponsored by the Wimberley Chamber of Commerce. (512) 847–2201.

November

- Pedal for the Planet, Austin. Benefits the Sierra Club. (512) 476–1889.

- Tour de Gruene, Gruene. Sponsored by the San Antonio Bicycle Racing Club. (210) 826–0177.

North Texas and the Piney Woods

March
- Possum Pedal 100, Graham. (817) 549–0780.
- Texas Dogwood Trails, Palestine. (903) 729–7275.

April
- Germanfest Metric Century Bicycle Rally, Muenster. (817) 759–2227.
- King's Cattle Trail Bike Ride, Lancaster. Benefit for Our Friends Place. (214) 373–2731.
- Mesquite Rodeo Ride, Mesquite. (214) 686–1477.
- Tour de Flowers, Corsicana. (903) 654–4840.

May
- Blackjack 100, Cumby. (903) 994–2211.
- Cowtown Classic, Ft. Worth. (817) 731–2922.
- Eagle 100K, Fort Worth. (817) 935–2979.
- MS 150 Bike Tour, Denton to Lake Murray, OK. (214) 373–1400.
- MADD'er than Hell, Denton. (817) 431–2231.
- The Rubicon, Longview. Sponsored by Good Shepherd Hospital. (903) 236–2049.
- Tour d'Arlington, Arlington. Benefits the Boys & Girls Clubs of Arlington. (817) 275–6551.

June
- Collin Classic, Plano. Benefits the Volunteer Center of Collin County. (800) 443–0946 or (214) 422–1050.
- Cow Creek Country Classic, Waxahachie. (214) 938–9827.
- Texas Chainring Challenge, Longview, seven-day tour. (800) 374–BIKE.
- Tour d'Italia, Italy. (214) 483–6198.

July

- Cycle to Recycle Bike Tour, Farmersville. (214) 475–1837.
- Peach Pedal, Weatherford. (817) 594–3801.
- Stephenville Firecracker 100 Bike Challenge, Stephenville. (817) 965–5313.

August

- Archer Scorcher, Archer. Sponsored by the Archer Chamber of Commerce. (817) 574–2489.
- Hot Rocks Bike Ride, Rockwall. (214) 772–4747.
- Hotter 'n Hell 100, Wichita Falls. (817) 692–2925.
- Keller Kountry Klassic, Keller. (817) 431–9011.
- Melon Patch Tour, Deleon. In conjunction with the Peach and Melon Festival. (817) 893–6600.

September

- Autumn in Bonham, Bonham. Sponsored by the Greater Dallas Bicyclists. (214) 946–BIKE.
- Beauty and the Beast, Tyler. (903) 533–1010.
- Bike the Rim, Glen Rose. (817) 897–2960.
- Bike to the Brazos, Fort Worth. Benefits the Multiple Sclerosis Society. (817) 496–4475.
- Grand Prairie Grand Prix, Grand Prairie. Sponsored by the Grand Prairie Chamber of Commerce. (800) 288–8386 or (214) 264–1558.
- Jackrabbit Stampede, Forney. (214) 564–2107.
- Tour de Possum, Texarkana. (903) 792–7380.

October

- Bethpage Mission Tornado Classic, Brownwood. Benefits persons with developmental disabilities. (915) 643–2944.
- Bowie Bash 100, Bowie. (817) 872–1173.
- Cedar Hill Annual Hilltop Classic, Cedar Hill. (214) 291–5300.
- Tornado Classic, Brownwood. (915) 643–2944.
- Tour de Fireant, Marshall. Sponsored by the Marshall Chamber of Commerce. (903) 935–7868.
- Tour de Pepper, Palestine. Sponsored by the Palestine Chamber of Commerce. (800) 659–3484.

Southeast Texas and the Gulf Coast

February
- Border Surf and Citrus 100, South Padre Island. Benefits the Shepherd's Center. (210) 423–3765.
- Frost Bike 50, Houston. Benefits the Arthritis Foundation. (800) 634–8000 or (713) 785–2360.

March
- Bicycle Around the Guadalupe (BRAG), Victoria. (800) 926–5774.
- Bluebonnet Metric Century, Hempstead. (713) 466–1240.

April
- Bluebonnet 50 Bike Ride, Washington-on-the-Brazos State Park. (713) 977–7706.
- Hurricane 100, near Houston. (713) 425–4891.
- San Antonio Shiner Ride, San Antonio to Shiner. (210) 493–8723.
- Tour de Cypress, Houston. (713) 466–1240.
- Wildflower Bike Outing, Cuero. Sponsored by the DeWitt County Wildflower Association. (512) 275–6303.

May
- Clean Air Challenge, Houston. Benefits the American Lung Association. (713) 629–LUNG.
- Great Escape 100, Huntsville. Sponsored by the Huntsville Chamber of Commerce. (800) 289–0389.
- MS 150 Bike Tour, Houston to Austin. Benefits the Multiple Sclerosis Society, two-day tour. (713) 526–8967 or (800) 323–4873.
- Mayflower 100, San Antonio. (210) 554–2648.
- Timberline Tour, Beaumont. (409) 838–3613.
- Wildflower 100 Bicycle Tour, San Antonio. Benefits Baptist Memorial Hospital. (210) 302–3075.

June

- Flapjack 50 Bike Ride, Houston. Benefits the American Diabetes Association. (713) 977–7706.
- Independence Challenge, Brenham, two-day tour. Benefits the American Lung Association. (713) 629–LUNG.

July

- Baytown Gator Race and Bike Tour, Baytown. (713) 421–1391.
- Hotter Than Ever Bicycle Classic, Beeville. Sponsored by the Bee County Chamber of Commerce. (512) 358–3267.
- Katy Flatland Century, Houston. (713) 466–1240.
- Tour de Braz, Alvin. Benefits the Mustang Bayou Bike and Hike Trail. (713) 331–3944.

September

- Bike to the Beach, San Antonio to Corpus Christi. Benefits the Multiple Sclerosis Society, two-day tour. (210) 494–5531 or (800) 683–1627.
- Crossroads Classic, Sealy. (713) 558–6211.
- Gulf Coast Century Classic Cycle Tour, Beaumont. Benefits the St. Elizabeth Hospital. (409) 838–3613.
- Pearl of the Prairie Bike Tour, El Campo. Sponsored by the El Campo Chamber of Commerce. (409) 543–1172.
- Pineywoods Purgatory, Lufkin. (409) 63–PEDAL.

October

- Annual Alamo Challenge Bike Trek, Houston to San Antonio. Benefits the American Lung Association. (713) 629–LUNG, ext. 109.
- D.E.B.R.A. Bike Tour, Brenham. Benefits the Dystrophic Epidermolysis Bullosa Research Association. (409) 836–0925.
- Houston Sierra Club Spin, Houston. (713) 798–5510.
- Missions Tour de Goliad, Goliad. Sponsored by the Goliad County Chamber of Commerce (800) 848–8674 or (512) 645–3565.

- Oktober Cycle–Fest, Galveston. Sponsored by the Knights of Columbus. (409) 744–1715.
- Road Runner Rally, South Padre Island. Rio Grande Valley Education Foundation. (800) 437–BIKE.
- Texas Coastal Cruise, Seabrook. (713) 798–5510.

West Texas and the Texas Panhandle

April
- Windrider Tours, Canyon. Benefits West Texas A & M University. (806) 499–3210.

May
- Land of High Sky Classic, Odessa. Sponsored by the Odessa East Rotary Club. (915) 561–8349.

June
- Sweetwater Fun Daze, 50K and 100K Race and Tour, Sweetwater. (800) 658–6757.
- Texas Double Trouble, Abilene. Benefits Mental Health Association and Abilene Regional MHMR Center. (915) 690–5137.

July
- Ride from the Border, Del Rio to San Angelo. Benefits the San Angelo Safe Kids Coalition. (915) 387–2880.

August
- Tour de Gap, Buffalo Gap. (915) 673–7415.

September
- Fort Davis Cyclefest, Fort Davis. Sponsored by the Permian Basin Bicycle Association. P.O. Box 60018, Midland, TX 79711.
- MDA Chili Pepper Pedal Century, El Paso. (915) 533–2632.
- Tour de Canyon, Crosbyton. Sponsored by the Crosbyton Chamber of Commerce. (806) 675–2261.

Appendix C

*Bicycle Clubs and Associations;
Cycling Advocacy Groups*

Riding with others can be a great way to enhance your enjoyment and knowledge of cycling. Bicycle clubs often sponsor organized rides and publish newsletters about happenings on the local cycling scene. Advocacy groups can be valuable sources of information and assistance on a broad range of cycling-related topics. A partial list of Texas bicycle clubs, associations, and advocacy groups follows.

Bicycle Clubs and Associations

Arlington Velo Club
P.O. Box 172546
Arlington, TX 76003
(817) 561–4427

Austin Cycling Association
P.O. Box 5993
Austin, TX 78763
(512) 477–0776

Caprock Bicycle Club
c/o Randy Stark, First National
  Bank
P.O. Box 540
Quitaque, TX 79225
(806) 455–1441

Carrollton Cycling Club
4019 Rive Lane
Addison, TX 75244
(214) 407–4477

Crossroads Cycling Club
P.O. Box 1844
Victoria, TX 77902

Fort Worth Bicycling Association
P.O. Box 534
Fort Worth, TX 76101
(817) 377–2457

Giddings Area Bicycle
  Association
P.O. Box 435
Giddings, TX 78942

Greater Dallas Bicyclists
P.O. Box 12822
Dallas, TX 75225
(214) 946–BIKE

Hill Country Cyclists
118 Kenwood
Boerne, TX 78006
(210) 249–8978

Houston Bicycle Club, Inc.
P.O. Box 52752
Houston, TX 77052
(713) 529–9709

Lone Star Cyclists
P.O. Box 532141
Grand Prairie, TX 75053
(214) 263–7411

Lubbock Bicycle Club
5728 76th Street
Lubbock, TX 79424

Permian Basin Bicycling
  Association
P.O. Box 60018
Midland, TX 79711

San Angelo Bicycling
  Association
P.O. Box 60942
San Angelo, TX 76906

San Antonio Wheelmen
Box 34208
San Antonio, TX 78265

Texarkana Bicycle Club
P.O. Box 7096
Texarkana, TX 75505

Ultra Marathon Cycling
  Association
P.O. Box 53
Canyon, TX 79015
(806) 499–3210

Violet Crown Sports Association
P.O. Box 3479
Austin, TX 78764
(512) 454–3255

Williamson County Cycling
  Club
P.O. Box 819
Round Rock, TX 78680
(512) 218–0879

Wichita Falls Bicycling Club
P.O. Box 2096
Wichita Falls, TX 76307
(817) 692–2925

Cycling Advocacy Groups

Adventure Cycling Association
P.O. Box 8308
Missoula, MT 59807
(406) 721–1776

Bicycle Federation of America
1506 21st Street NW, Suite 200
Washington, DC 20036
(202) 463–6622

Bicycle Information Committee
Texas Committee on Natural
  Resources
5934 Royal Lane, Suite 223
Dallas, TX 75206
(214) 368–1791

City of Austin
Department of Public Works
  and Transportation
Bicycle Service Line
505 Barton Springs Road, #850
Austin, TX 78704
(512) 480–0370

City of Dallas Department of
  Transportation
Bicycle Program Coordinator
1500 Marilla, 5C-S
Dallas, TX 75201
(214) 670–4039

Houston Area Bicyclist Alliance
P.O. Box 25372
Houston, TX 77265
(713) 729–9333

League of American Bicyclists
190 W. Olmstead Street, Suite
  120
Baltimore, MD 21230
(410) 539–3496

Rails-to-Trails Conservancy
1400 16th Street NW, Suite 300
Washington, DC 20036
(202) 797–5400

State Bicycle/Pedestrian
  Coordinator
Texas Department of
  Transportation
125 E. 11th Street
Austin, TX 78701
(512) 416–3125

Texas Bicycle Coalition
P.O. Box 1121
Austin, TX 78767
(512) 476–7433

United States Cycling
  Federation
One Olympic Plaza
Colorado Springs, CO
(719) 578–4581

Women's Cycling Coalition
P.O. Box 281
Louisville, CO 80027
(303) 666–0500

Appendix D

Route Index

Mileage, starting points, and parks featured along each route are listed below.

The right-hand column provides mileage for each option detailed in the corresponding route description. Fully half of the fifty routes in this book have at least one additional distance option.

Next to the title of each route, in parentheses, is the city or town where the ride starts and finishes, followed by the county where the ride starts and finishes. Several rides cross one or more county lines during their course.

Listed beneath the title of each route is any state or national park facility visited on the route. Other parks near, but not actually on, the course of a route are not listed. Also not listed are the many county, local, and private park facilities passed on the route, and the many buildings and sites listed on the state or national Registers of Historic Places.

There are twenty-two state parks, forests, natural areas, and historic sites; four national parks and historic sites; three national forests; two national wildlife refuges; and a national seashore listed below.

Central Texas and the Hill Country

	Miles
1. Garven's Store Classic (Hunt/Kerr)	67.2
2. Lost Maples Challenge (Vanderpool/Bandera)	49.4
■ **Lost Maples State Natural Area**	
3. Bandera Classic (Bandera/Bandera)	73.9
4. Kerr County Cruise (Kerrville/Kerr)	33.2
■ **Kerrville-Schreiner State Park**	

	Miles
5. The Sawicki's Favorite Hill Country Challenge (Fredericksburg/Gillespie)	53.5
6. Willow City Ramble (Willow City/Gillespie)	21.3
7. Luckenbach Cruise (Fredericksburg or Luckenbach/Gillespie)	37.2/13.2
8. LBJ Country Cruise (Stonewall/Gillespie)	36.5/21.7
■ Lyndon B. Johnson State and National Historical Parks	
9. Two Gruene/River Road Cruises (Gruene/Comal)	34.9/30.7
10. Devil's Backbone Cruise (Wimberley/Hays)	28.8
11. Wimberley Metric Century Classic (Wimberley/Hays)	61.7
12. Lost Pines Cruise (Bastrop/Bastrop)	37.2/30.8
■ Bastrop State Park; Buescher State Park	
13. Pflugerville Farm Country Challenge (Pflugerville/Travis)	50.0/37.1/17.7
14. Two Salado Rambles (Salado/Bell)	30.7/23.0
15. Hill Country Flyer Challenge (Burnet/Burnet)	56.2/29.0
16. Longhorn Caverns Cruise (Burnet/Burnet)	39.9/33.9/27.2
■ Inks Lake State Park; Longhorn Caverns State Park	

North Texas and the Piney Woods

17. Possum Kingdom Challenge (Caddo*/Stephens)	48.9
■ Possum Kingdom State Park	
18. Palo Pinto Ramble (Palo Pinto/Palo Pinto)	28.5
19. Granbury Cruise (Granbury/Hood)	41.7/36.4
20. Dinosaur Valley Ramble (Glen Rose/Somervell)	27.1/15.1
■ Dinosaur Valley State Park	
21. White Rock Ramble (Dallas/Dallas)	23.2
22. Autumn Trails Ramble (Winnsboro/Wood)	28.9/16.0
23. Caddo Lake Cruise (Jefferson/Marion)	33.5
■ Caddo Lake State Park	
24. Lake O' the Pines Ramble (Jefferson/Marion)	26.5

		Miles
25.	Tyler Rose Classic (Tyler/Smith)	71.0/52.3/48.8/30.1
26.	Palestine Challenge	50.2/23.8
	(Palestine/Anderson)	
27.	Texas State Railroad Challenge	38.7/21.7
	(Rusk/Cherokee)	
	▪ **Rusk State Park; I. D. Fairchild State Forest**	
28.	El Camino Real Challenge (Alto/Cherokee)	49.0/40.4
	▪ **Caddoan Mounds State Historical Park,**	
	Mission Tejas State Historical Park	
29.	San Augustine Cruise	41.2/31.4
	(San Augustine/San Augustine)	
	▪ **Angelina National Forest**	

Southeast Texas and the Gulf Coast

30.	San Antonio Missions Ramble (San Antonio/Bexar)	14.3
	▪ **San Antonio Missions**	
	National Historical Park	
31.	La Bahia Challenge (Goliad/Goliad)	51.0/34.7/27.4
32.	Laguna Atascosa Challenge	52.4/33.0/14.4
	(Port Isabel/Cameron)	
	▪ **Laguna Atascosa National Wildlife Refuge**	
33.	South Padre Island Ramble	24.4
	(South Padre Island/Cameron)	
	▪ **Padre Island National Seashore**	
34.	Big Thicket Challenge	46.5/40.2/19.5
	(Kountze/Hardin)	
	▪ **Big Thicket National Preserve**	
35.	Palmetto Cruise (Gonzales/Gonzales)	32.9
	▪ **Palmetto State Park**	
36.	Groveton/Davy Crockett National Forest Cruise	37.4
	(Groveton/Trinity)	
	▪ **Davy Crockett National Forest**	
37.	Two Coldspring Rambles	30.7/24.3/18.2
	(Coldspring/San Jacinto)	
	▪ **Sam Houston National Forest**	

	Miles
38. Grimes County Cruise (Anderson/Grimes)	35.2/22.0
39. Washington-on-the-Brazos Challenge (Chappell Hill/Washington)	41.9/21.0/13.2
■ **Washington-on-the-Brazos State Park**	
40. Blue Bell Ramble (Brenham/Washington)	29.6
41. Austin's Colony Cruise (Fayetteville/Fayette)	35.4
42. Round Top Ramble (Round Top/Fayette)	29.2/21.0

West Texas and the Texas Panhandle

43. Buffalo Gap Cruise (Buffalo Gap/Taylor)	28.0
■ **Abilene State Park**	
44. Rails–to–Trails Ramble (Quitaque/Briscoe)	18.2
■ **Caprock Canyons State Park**	
45. Palo Duro Canyon Cruise (Canyon*/Randall)	15.3
■ **Palo Duro Canyon State Park**	
46. Panhandle Plains Challenge (Canyon/Randall)	55.3/45.3/40.5/30.5
■ **Buffalo Lake National Wildlife Refuge**	
47. Davis Mountains Classic (Fort Davis/Jeff Davis)	75.4
■ **Davis Mountains State Park; Fort Davis National Historic Site**	
48. *Giant* Classic (Fort Davis/Jeff Davis)	71.4
49. Two Chisos Mountain Challenges (Big Bend National Park*/Brewster)	48.0/40.8/19.2
■ **Big Bend National Park**	
50. El Camino del Rio Classic (Terlingua*/Brewster)	100.0
■ **Big Bend Ranch State Natural Area**	
■ **Fort Leaton State Historical Site**	

Since the starting point of the Possum Kingdom Challenge, Palo Duro Canyon Cruise, Two Chisos Mountain Challenges, and El Camino del Rio Classic are park grounds, mailing addresses are used. Possum Kingdom State Park is actually 16 miles from Caddo across the Palo Pinto County line. Big Bend Ranch State Natural Area is actually 1 mile east of Lajitas and 2 miles east of the Presidio County line.

About the Author

Andy White's first touring bicycle was a white Raleigh ten-speed with black trim. He bought it in 1972, to ride to summer jobs in the Hudson River Valley of New York State. The bicycle went with him to college, where he developed an enduring passion for cycling on long rides through the pine forests of North Carolina. Andy first visited the Texas Hill Country in 1975, and the Raleigh ten-speed first traveled in Texas along the roads described in Jeff Garvey's Favorite Hill Country Challenge. After moving to Austin, Andy continued to explore Texas by bicycle, although the Raleigh ten-speed was eventually reduced to spare parts. Several bicycles later, Andy has logged over forty thousand miles on cycling trips throughout Texas, as well as thirty other states and six countries.

Also of interest from The Globe Pequot Press

Quick Escapes from Dallas/Fort Worth 30 Weekend Getaways in East Texas	$13.95
Daytrips from Houston, 6th Edition Getaways less than two hours away from the city	$11.95
Texas: Off the Beaten Path A guide to unique places	$11.95

Other books in this Series:

The Best Bike Rides in the Mid-Atlantic	$12.95
The Best Bike Rides in the New England	$12.95
The Best Bike Rides in the Midwest	$12.95
The Best Bike Rides in the South	$12.95
The Best Bike Rides in California	$12.95
The Best Bike Rides in the Pacific Northwest	$12.95

Available from your bookstore or directly from
the publisher. For a free catalogue or to place an order,
call toll-free 24 hours a day (1–800–243–0495),
or write to The Globe Pequot Press, P.O. Box 833,
Old Saybrook, Connecticut 06475–0833.